A Tenderfoot Kid on Gyp Water

Carl P. Benedict, 1895

By CARL PETERS BENEDICT

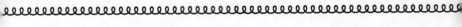

A Tenderfoot Kid
on
Gyp Water

Illustrated

Introduction by J. FRANK DOBIE

University of Nebraska Press
Lincoln and London

First Bison Book printing: 1986
Most recent printing indicated by the first digit below:
1   2   3   4   5   6   7   8   9   10

Library of Congress Cataloging-in-Publication Data
Benedict, Carl Peters.
   A tenderfoot kid on gyp water.
   "Bison book" —verso t.p.
   Reprint. Originally published: Austin: Texas
Folklore Society, 1943. (Range life series)
   1. Benedict, Carl Peters. 2. Cowboys—Texas—
Biography. 3. Ranch life—Texas. 4. Texas—
Social life and customs. 5. Texas—Biography.
I. Title.
F391.B487 1986   976.4'06'0924   86-6911
ISBN 0-8032-6079-2 (pbk.)

Originally published in 1943 by the Texas Folklore Society, Austin,
Texas, and the University Press, Dallas, Texas

DEDICATED

to the memory of Cap Weatherly, a cowpuncher who worked for the Figure 8 outfit in the spring of 1894, long since gone by; a natural philosopher who met the troubles of life with a kindly wit and humor that made the trail brighter for this tenderfoot kid. He was my first friend in the old chuck wagon days.

CARL P. BENEDICT

Odessa, Texas   January, 1933

CONTENTS

ILLUSTRATIONS

INTRODUCTION

By J. Frank Dobie

In 1841 the Republic of Texas entered into a contract with W. S. Peters, of Louisville, Kentucky, and associates to settle 600 colonists in Texas. Married settlers were to be granted a section of land each, unmarried settlers a half-section, and the colonizers themselves ten sections for every one hundred colonists brought in. In subsequent years the Peters contract was extended and modified. The Peters colony on the Trinity River had a history not happy.

In 1877 H. J. Peters, son of the colonizer, set out from Kentucky to settle on Peters Company land. It was west of the old Peters colony; it was on the frontier. In the wagons with H. J. Peters and his wife and two sons came his daughter, Mrs. Adele Peters Benedict, and her two sons, Harry Yandell, born in 1869, and Carl Peters, born in 1874. The father and husband, Joseph E. Benedict, had preceded the family migration and established a small ranch near Fort Belknap in Young County. He had fought for four years in the Confederate Army and risen from private to captain. In Texas everybody knew him affectionately as "Cap." In love of horses at least, Carl was to take strongly after him, while Harry Yandell, though a great lover and student of nature, was to take more after his mother.

The Peters family, the Benedicts continuing to live with them, located on a half section of land fronting the Clear Fork of the Brazos River. The big house they built out of lumber freighted from Fort Worth was in time found to be exactly bisected by the line separating Young and Stephens Counties. The few cattle they had they were for a long time afraid to turn out of the pens at night for fear the cowboys would drive them off. With great labor they built a rock fence around part of their land. They grubbed mesquite from and plowed up land utterly worthless for anything but grazing. The country was, and still is, mostly a ranch country. It was not fenced until "bob" wire came in years after the arrival of the Benedicts.

Graham, in Young County, where cattlemen in 1876 organized what is now nationally known as the Texas and Southwestern Cattle Raisers Association, was the trading point. Coming out of Graham one day in a hack, Carl Benedict and others of the family heard yells and shots and, looking back, saw six cowboys tearing down the road, "riding like drunk Indians." The hack was pulled to one side to give them a clear passage. Carl wanted to be a cowboy.

The wagons had brought a thousand good books from Kentucky. Mrs. Benedict read to her boys, taught them. They went to school in Graham a winter. For four winters Carl rode horseback to a little school at Eliasville. Meantime Harry Yandell (H. Y.) was studying farther afield, taking the road that led him to a Ph.D. from Harvard, then to professorship, deanship and finally presidency at the University of Texas. "My mother and Yandell sent me to Austin one year," Carl Benedict remembers, "but I hated to live there so bad and loved the home

Mrs. Carl P. Benedict, bride of 18, in 1898

place and the cattle and horses so much that I begged
them to let me stay at home the next year. I told them
that if they would let me stay at home I would learn
to cook biscuits for my mother, who was sick and not
able to cook. She died in November of 1894, my
father having preceded her. We were very sad for a
long time after that. The spring and summer before
this, however, were perhaps the happiest time of my
life, the cowboy days on the open range about which
I have written my book."

In 1898 Carl P. Benedict married eighteen-years-
old Mamie Caudle, from Haskell County. Six years
later they went farther west and "fought sandstorms
and drouths for thirty years, went broke twice and
raised our children, got on our feet again." One of
these children, the youngest, Carl P., Jr., had been in
the Naval Air Service for nearly fourteen years and
was at Cavite when the Japs took it. He got out of
Corregidor in a submarine and made it to Australia.
The second boy, Ed, works at the bomber plant near
Fort Worth. The oldest son, Norman, ranches near
Melrose, New Mexico.

In the spring of 1933 I was in the cow and oil town
of Midland, Texas, to make a commencement speech.
Death will have no added sting for me if I never make
another. The morning after it was over I was having
a bully time talking to some of the old-timers—Bill
Gates, who while poisoning prairie dogs once saw an
old rattlesnake on the edge of a dog hole swallow a
passell of little ones; Brooks Lee, who drove a herd
to California in 1869; hearty Spence Jowell, and

others. Then I met a little grey man whose features
and behavior showed that he had spent many steady
years on drouthy ranges without ever making enough
money to speak of and also without having let adver-
sity dim out the bright spark of life that nature had
lighted for him long before he was born. He was
very shy and diffident in turning over to me a manuscript that a Texas printer had offered to publish if
somebody would pay for the printing. He had a vague
and very modest idea that I might interest a "real
publisher" in putting it out.

Even at first sight the little grey, shy man did not
seem a stranger to me. He looked like and in many
ways reminded me of his brother, H. Y. Benedict,
whom I had known many years and whom I loved
and also not infrequently disagreed with. I read the
manuscript with pleasure, and even though it needed
revising, thought it worthy of a publisher's consideration. No publisher that I offered it to, however,
agreed with me. I have read plenty of range narra-
tives from their presses that seem to me less valid and
vital.

In a way, C. P. Benedict was greatly relieved that
his narrative was not published. He had trepidations
lest the publication of this plain story of an "ordinary
cowpuncher" might embarrass his distinguished
brother, not only president of the University of Texas
but one of the best known and best loved citizens of
Texas. "Benny," as thousands called Doctor Benedict, was one of the most natural men that ever lived,
and he and his brother were dear to each other. He
realized that the book could not make anybody any

money, but the intelligence, sense of humor, rightness
of heart, observant sympathy for nature and gentle
sensitiveness manifest throughout *A Tenderfoot Kid
on Gyp Water* would have pleased him, I am sure.

This narrative is not a man's life story. It is com-
posed of memories of but a single season of his golden
youth. It shows how memories, like rhetoric, solace
mankind. "Some of my most vivid recollections,"
Carl Benedict wrote me ten years ago, "have come at
odd moments and then been forgotten before I had a
chance to write them down." He did not write for
solace.

Last fall while he was selling out his stock of cattle
in the Odessa country and giving up a lease on a
small ranch, he confessed in a letter: "I wrote my
book during the most unhappy period of my life. I
was badly broke and had a wild hope that it would
make me some money. The old ball faces [white-
faced Herefords] that I stuck with have made me
more than I ever could have got out of the book, even
if it had been published by a promoter. . . . When I
think how long we have struggled on through the
sandstorms and drouths and low prices, it seems like
a dream with no ending."

Three weeks later, having delivered his ranch and
gone with Mrs. Benedict on a visit to Chillicothe,
Texas, the old cowpuncher wrote: "So many army
camps and so many people, we may go back to Odessa
to live. Might not last long and hate to leave the Cow
Country anyway. Can't stand so many people." Now
they are in Fort Worth, figuring on buying a house
and settling down there. But no man who has lived

his life on a ranch ever gets over the "too many people" of a town.

Any reader has a right to know what an editor has done to a piece of writing published under another man's name. Many a writer seeing his work in print after editorial exercise could well exclaim with the old woman in Mother Goose, "Laws a me, this is none of I." Well, though I have changed hundreds of commas to periods, reparagraphed, cut out excess words, and now and then revamped a sentence, the Kid is still himself—"none of I"—just Carl Benedict.

Austin, Texas

June 3, 1943

Chapter I

North Texas Range in 1894

In 1894, NEARLY ALL THE LAND between the timber in Central Texas and the Cap Rock on the east side of the Plains was unfenced, except for a few large ranches like the Matador, Pitchfork, Spur, Figure 8, and, farther south, the S M S, of the Swensons. These companies owned a lot of land, had fenced it and established permanent headquarters. Some of the other large outfits and many small operators owned only enough land apiece to establish a camp on, while they ran thousands of cattle on the unfenced range. They were the men who vigorously argued that a man could not make a cent out of cattle in Texas unless he got the grass for nothing. How much this opinion has changed could be seen by looking on the account checks of some present-day owners. In 1894, some of the large established ranches ran lots of cattle on "the outside," as they called the unfenced country, and most of them ran a wagon, or "outfit," through April until late in the fall, branding calves and gathering dry cows and steers they wanted to ship or sell.

When these wagons started out in the spring, all the small cowmen who could not afford to run a wagon themselves would either go or send one of their own boys or a hired cowboy, with a mount of horses and a bed roll, packed on one of the horses, to work with the wagon and gather the little brands of cattle they owned and bring them back to the home ranch. These little cowmen, sifting in among and alongside the big ranches, which usually brought no families, were the first real settlers of the country. The little cowman came with his family, a few cattle, horses, and the "woman's" chickens in a little coop, tied on the wagon.

All the boys who did not work for the cattle company that owned the roundup wagon were called "stray men"; the boys who worked for the big companies were called "company men," Figure 8 men, O X men, etc. Each roundup wagon carried a coil of large rope, about one and a half inches in diameter, to make hobbles out of. It was customary to hobble all horses at night, except each man's night horse, which was saddled and kept staked, ready for the puncher to mount when it came his time to go on guard.

I think it was Cal Lowry, the cook for the 8 outfit, who taught me how to make rope hobbles. In each three-ply strand of rope there is a little strand in the center, which can be plainly seen when the rope is cut into hobble lengths. If this center strand is pulled out of each hobble before the knot is tied in the end, the hobble will get very soft and pliable after a few days' use and will not chafe the horse's ankles. Should the puncher neglect to pull out this center strand and also fail to stretch his hobble rope before tying the knots in it, it would remain hard and probably skin up the horse's ankles the first time heavy dew or rain caused the hobble rope to shrink.

When camp was made for the night, it was the wrang's [horse wrangler's] duty to have the horses rounded up near the wagon. When the men got in from the herd, some of them would scatter around the horses, holding ropes about waist high from the ground, making a rope corral. Other men would go into the rope corral and rope out the night horses, tying them out of the way. When all the night horses were caught, the men not holding the ropes for the corral would then creep in amongst the loose horses and hobble each one securely around the fore-legs. It was surprising to see a wild horse stand and let a man walk up and put the hobbles on him. The horses were so crowded up together in the rope corral that they could hardly see the men creeping around and putting the hobbles on them. Some of the young broncs had to be caught, but they got used to the hobbling process in a very short time.

Although many outfits no longer hobble, hobbling makes horses gentle and keeps them near camp. In a good grass country, hobbled horses can fill up quickly. Horses always graze at night. When morning came the hobbles were taken off the horses and tied around their necks. If a wild cow or calf ran off from the roundup and would not come back, the hobble was a mighty good thing to tie it down with. I have seen many a cowboy spread his loop on a wild one while running his horse at full speed, throw it, jerk the hobble off his horse's neck, run to the end of his rope and tie the brute almost as quick as it hit the ground.

It was generally understood that if any cowboy had to rope a wild cow, a calf, or an ordinary-sized steer to keep it from quitting the drive or the roundup, that was this man's job alone, and no one paid any attention to him. The animal that was tied down lay where it was tied until they could bring the drive up to it or until they got through working the roundup, when some gentle cattle would be driven to where the brute was tied. Then the men would untie it among the other cattle and let it get up and go off with them. If one of the big wild steers quit the drive, two men would usually go after him, as this was hard and dangerous work. If a big steer was "on the prod," both men would rope him around the horns to keep him from goring one of the horses before he could be tied down.

Before starting on the drive each morning, the boss would tell the cook where to camp the wagon for dinner that day. Two or three men would load the bedding on the wagon, while another man helped the cook hitch up four mules. Each cowboy was supposed to keep his bed properly rolled up and tied with a rope, or with two good leather straps, so it could be handled and pitched up in the wagon without coming untied. Two or three men would be detailed to help move the herd to the next camp with the wagon and horses, while the rest of the outfit would make the drive with the boss, throwing the cattle together at the next camp.

Sometimes the wagon would not be moved after the morning drive, and the evening would be spent branding calves. When we were to brand, the day herd would be rounded up on an open place. Then two riders would go into it to rope the calves and drag them to the fire, where the rest of the crew would throw them down, take off the ropes, and hold them for the men to mark, brand and castrate. It requires a skilful roper to work in a herd on the prairie, and only the top hands can do it. A roper has to be certain he knows the brand on the calf's mother, and he calls this out to the branding crew when he drags the calf up—to prevent mistakes in ownership.

The roper picks a gentle horse, one that will prowl through the cattle without blowing his nose, champing on the bits, or slinging his head, which disturbs the herd and makes them restless. Some horses have nerves, just like people. They are afraid of a rope and will do their best to keep the roper from getting a throw. Jim Nash, an old hand on the range, once told me he was at a roundup on the "outside" near the little town of Aspermont, where he saw Ed Lanier (one of the best range ropers) ride in the herd and catch 163 calves before he missed a throw. There were few pens and no chutes to speak of in those days, and the country from the Texas & Pacific Railway north to the Texas line was worked almost entirely by white men. There were no Mexicans east of the plains in that region, and few Negroes. Hardly any one carried a gun. If a stray man rode up to the wagon with a gun belted on him, the boss usually told him to leave it at the wagon, until he got ready to cut his cattle and take them home.

In going on guard at night, hardly any cowboy wore leather leggins, because they would be in the way and fastening the snaps to put them on and take them off would require too much time, especially as the operations had to be in the dark, or at best, in the light of the cook's lantern, which hung at the back end of the wagon every dark night. To save time and trouble every man wore his spurs on his boots day and night, never taking them off. His spurs came off only with his boots. It took just a few seconds for the puncher to slip on his pants, boots, and coat and take his night horse off the stake rope. He would be at the herd, ready to let the other boys come in, very soon after crawling out of his pallet. There was practically only one kind of spur used then; it was the OK brand, a small, close-fitting spur, made in the two-button style. They could be easily slipped up on the heel, so as to loosen the instep, when a puncher pulled his boots off to go to bed.

Nearly every one in that country used the S. C. Gallup saddle, made at Pueblo, Colorado. It was a small, heavy saddle, built with a low fork and either broad or narrow seat. It was strong for roping on and riding wild horses. It could be used equally well with one or two girts. Everything was cheap then, and a dandy good saddle could be bought for thirty-five to forty dollars, a pair of spurs with leathers for two dollars, a good slicker for three dollars, and bridle with bits complete for from two to four dollars. Local blacksmiths made good strong hand-made bits at from two to three dollars without any mounting. I do not remember seeing any Navaho blankets in those times, though the top hand generally paid more for the blanket than for any other part of his rig, except the saddle. Many punchers paid eight to ten dollars for the best wool blankets they could find, mostly bright red or blue. Folded properly, with an old piece of blanket under them for a sweat pad, they made good protection for the horse's back. Likewise, many of the men would buy a pair or two of fine wool blankets for their beds. With two or three heavy quilts, two pair of ten-dollar blankets, a "goose hair" pillow and a good tarpaulin, to roll the bed up in and to pull over his head, if he had a chance to sleep when it rained, the puncher of that day thought himself pretty well hooked up for cow work.

Chapter II

The Figure 8 Wagon

IN THE SPRING OF 1894, the Louisville Land and Cattle Company sent a cow outfit from their headquarters ranch, in King County, Texas, to a point about eighteen miles southeast of Childress, to gather and bring home about 2500 head of stock cattle they had moved there the year before to winter on the fine grass in the Pease River breaks. As the company branded the figure 8 lying down on both hips, on their horses and cattle, their wagon was called the Figure 8 Wagon. Their ear mark on cattle, as I recall, was underslope on the left ear.

Having grown up in the settlements, as the cowboys called the country in central Texas, I had never done any real cow work, but knew enough about it to be crazy to get away and work on the range with the big outfits. Finally getting a job with two men who made their headquarters near a little town called Raynor, in Western Texas, I was sent with one of the owner's sons to work with the 8 Wagon on the Pease River range that summer of 1894. These men had turned some cattle loose on that range the preceding fall and wished to gather and sell them, or bring them back to the Double Mountain country. Taking two mounts of horses (18 head) and a bed roll each, packed on one of the horses, we set out for the Figure 8 Ranch. The manager had agreed to let us go north and work with their wagon that summer, for while we were gathering our cattle, we could help the 8's gather theirs at no additional expense except the chuck bill. My companion's name was Will Lanier. He was the oldest son of W. T. Lanier, a well-known stockman in that part of the west. We got to the 8 Ranch late one evening, and Will made me acquainted with Mr. Arnett, the boss of the whole ranch, with Cal Lowry, the cook for the wagon, and with some of the cow-punchers.

The Figure 8 Ranch was located on a hill, on the north side of a dry creek that had water holes some distance apart in it, although they did not last except during the rainy season. The manager lived in a nice frame cottage on the hill. His family used water from a cistern, dug in the ground and cemented, that was supplied by gutters on the house to catch rainwater from the roof. The hands lived in a bunk-house near the corrals. A store-house, a small barn near the corrals, was filled with ranch supplies of all kinds, and there was a blacksmith shop, where they kept tools to shoe horses and do other kinds of ranch work. In this storehouse, also, the men kept their saddles and other junk. There was a large tank, made by putting an earthern dam across the creek just south of the ranch buildings, that they told me never went dry. There were cross fences through this tank built so the cattle and horses could water there from four dif-ferent small pastures or traps. The traps allowed plenty of room for 100 head or more of saddle horses, for holding a herd of cattle for a short time, for milk cows, etc.

The extra, and also the steady, hands lived at the

bunk-house and used the tank water for drinking as well as for all other uses. It was rain water and did not taste "gyppy" like the "live" water holes in the creeks that were fed by springs. Most of these springs were in the gyp rock canyons, and were so strong they tasted like a half and half solution of epsom salts and quinine. No one ever went back to get another drink out of a "gyp" water hole, unless nearly crazed by thirst. Sometimes that summer when the cook would run out of rain water in the barrels carried in the front end of the wagon, we tried not drinking anything but coffee, but the coffee, while not so bitter with sugar in it as the creek and spring water, would have the same effect on one's innards. The water that ran into the dirt tanks, from rains that fell in the hill country, was considered the best water to be had, except cistern water. When the cistern at the house went dry, the ranch people would gladly drink tank water, which they hauled to the house in barrels, until the next rains came.

The boss and Cal Lowry were older men than the other hands, and the boss had a certain air of dignity and a steady look in his clear grey eyes that made me wish I could be a man like him some day. I got used to the cook first. Cowboys generally try to make friends with cooks. It was quite natural for a new man to want to know where the cook kept the lick (syrup), sugar and other delicacies, which skillet the beef and gravy were in, and where the hot biscuits were. By a careful study and good recollection of these things, with due regard for the cook's desire to be treated considerately around the wagon, a puncher can make friends with almost any cook; but if a puncher hangs around the fire on a cold morning, gets in the way, and gives up too much "head" while the cook is trying to get breakfast for fifteen or twenty men, it is a cinch that puncher will not get any dough-nuts hid away in a bucket for special occasions.

There were eight or ten men in the bunk-house when we went in there that evening. They all worked for the 8 outfit, and were strangers to me, though my companion knew and had worked with them all. Be-ing somewhat timid, I could feel the hair rise on my head, while standing in there among them. To my youthful eyes, they were the most dangerous and fiercest set of men I had ever got mixed up with. They were talking and laughing among themselves, and paid little attention to me. Being a kid, their fierce oaths, the wild talk of the cow country, the tales of fights, bad men, bad horses and bad women, all made the cold shivers run up and down my back. However, after I looked timidly around, I concluded they might be like the "devil" who, according to the old story, "is not so black as he is painted." In fact, this outfit was as fine a bunch of men as any boss could want to start out with on a trip, though some of them were like the horses they rode—"they would not do to monkey with."

The next morning Will Lanier and myself, having nothing to do until the outfit got ready to start, found an old man at the ranch who knew how to call turkeys and went with him on horse back up in the brush, three or four miles. That country was hilly with little round mottes of scrub hackberry and cedar bushes,

which made lots of protection and shelter for wild
game as well as wild cattle. Having found a likely
place to call, we tied our horses off some distance, the
old man located himself in a clump of bushes and hid
us two boys behind him. It seemed just a few minutes
before a large gobbler came in sight. Will, who had
borrowed the only rifle on the ranch, a forty-four
Winchester, opened fire. At the first shot the turkey
turned and ran, Will running after him shooting as he
ran. All at once the big bird tumbled over. The 8
boys had a fine gobbler for dinner the next day.

The most important man with our outfit was Mr.
Bud Arnett, the wagon boss. He had an extra good
mount of horses; his bed roll was about like that of
any cowboy. There were no automobiles then, and
the manager of a ranch would often take charge of a
wagon and work on the outside range for two or three
months at the busy season of the year, sometimes
staying with the wagon until it got through work in
the fall, riding horseback to the home ranch once in a
while to look after things, though one or two trusted
men were always left at headquarters. Mr. Arnett
was a large man, strongly built, with sandy hair, a
stubby mustache, grey eyes and light complexion. He
was quiet in his ways, though sometimes when the
boys would get to swearing at their horses, or the
blankety-blank rope that kinked up so you could not
throw it in the creek, the boss would look around with
a smile and ask who the peeler was that was "cussin"
so loud. Then everyone would laugh and go to telling
jokes. It was whispered around camp that the boss
was a church member. I do not know about that. He

never swore himself, and every one liked him. One thing was certain: All men working with Bud Arnett's wagon were treated alike; he had no favorites. He would not allow gambling or drinking around the wagon.

Next to the boss, in some minds was the cook, and no better one ever went out on the range than Cal Lowry, who cooked for the 8's that summer. A tall, thin, handsome man, of middle age, with brown eyes and a long drooping mustache, he was an expert cook and also a dandy good man. He told me lots of things about the work that helped me out. When Will Lanier and I went to work with the 8's that spring, I was a miserable little runt of a human, about nineteen years old, and it crowded me to weigh 115 pounds with my boots and spurs on. But after working three or four months outdoors, sleeping on the ground every night, and eating Cal Lowry's hot rolls and Figure 8 beef, with thick gravy, plenty of "lick" or stewed prunes to wind up on, three times a day, I felt like a different human, in a new carcass. The hard work and riding day and night got easy for me.

The horse wrangler was named George Ratliff, a younger brother of Bud and Dor Ratliff, who had a ranch in King County. Marion McGinty was the bronc rider for the outfit, a medium-sized, slim-built youngster about twenty years of age, with light hair, blue eyes, and fair skin. He moved with such ease and quickness, even in his boots and spurs, that a casual observer would class him as one of the type who shined on the floor of the big cow-town dances they used to have, though a close look, when he handled a wild horse, showed he was a real "peeler." He could saddle a mean bronc, by himself, with more ease than some men can saddle the ordinary horse.

Cap Weatherly, his brother Harry, Ross Sloan, called "Tige" for short, and Bruce Wheeler were with the wagon when it started, besides Will Lanier and myself. Tom Davidson and one or two more of the company men were already up there on the Pease River range. These were all Figure 8 men except Will and myself. While George Ratliff, Will Lanier, "Tige" Sloan, and Marion McGinty were all about my age, they were seasoned hands and knew the range work from start to finish.

On the morning of April 10, 1894, two men caught the cook's four mules and helped him hitch up the loaded wagon. It pulled out north. Behind it the "wrang" (horse wrangler), with the help of another man, drove the saddle horses. The rest of us just rode along together. That was a rainy spring, and we hadn't more than got started before the rain came down in sheets. I had on my coat and had a slicker tied on my saddle. McGinty had left his coat and slicker both in the wagon. I loaned him my coat and wore the slicker.

The boss traveled at orderly speed. He never got in a hurry, and he was always on time. If any of the men had trouble with a mean horse at leaving camp, the wagon pulled out anyway, just as if nothing was going on, though another man would usually stay with the man having trouble until he could ride the "pitch" out of his horse and catch up with the wagon. Mr. Arnett, whose home was at Benjamin, in Knox

County, had been boss of the 8 Ranch for several years. He afterwards became general manager of the Louisville Land and Cattle Company. Though operating in Texas, the home office was in Louisville, Kentucky.

This ranch contained, to the best of my recollection, 125,000 acres of land that the company owned in fee. It was all fenced. Most of the land was in the rough, cedar hill country, south and east of the little county seat called Guthrie. There was nothing much there in the way of a town then, and I remember one night, while we were on guard, how Cap Weatherly confided to me that he owned fifteen or twenty lots in Guthrie, part of them "business lots," and offered to sell me all or part of them, with a clear title, as he said he did not owe a damn nickel on them, for a consideration of $5 per lot. I do not know whether the company had any leased land fenced in with their other land or not, but they ran several thousand cattle on that ranch. It was rough and hilly, but an awful good cow country. This ranch was afterwards sold to S. B. Burnett, of Fort Worth, and Bud Arnett remained in charge as general manager for long years after the property changed hands.

Chapter III

McGinty and Dynamite

ON THIS TRIP NORTH with the Figure 8 outfit the first duty of a cowpuncher, as I learned, was to wake up early. A heavy sleeper gets little sympathy in a cow camp. I got up promptly when the cook put the bread on to bake, as it would be done and ready to eat by the time I could dress, roll up my bed, wash my face and comb my hair. Most of the boys never got up till the cook called them, but, being a new hand and a little slow, I gave myself more time.

The cowboys I worked with that summer were not the dirty, lousy, ignorant people sometimes pictured as cowpunchers. We all carried two or three sets of clean underclothes, shirts, and a new pair of pants, tied up in a flour sack, which also contained a razor and shaving material. Some of the top hands carried a little grip, instead of a flour sack, rolled up in their beds. There were plenty of places to bathe, as one could take a bath in the gyp water pools, which became as clear as a crystal when the water settled in them after a rain, or we could take a bath in the fresh water holes that were common, both on the prairies and in the hills, when it rained. We could also wash our own clothes at these water holes, or take them to a laundry woman, when the wagon got to the railroad. None of these men used the slow drawl in their talk. Most of them could talk very good grammar school language, and most of them were lively and quick witted. They had to be quick in thought and action, because they daily matched their wits against the mean horses they rode and the wild cattle they worked with.

One morning after breakfast when the horses were rounded up to start on the day's journey north, two or three head were missing out of the bunch. While looking around, Mr. Arnett happened to see Mc- Ginty, the bronc peeler, standing near, and told him to take me with him, go back and get the lost horses and bring them back to the outfit, while they moved on. A heavy-loaded chuck-wagon, piled high with a lot of beds on top, cannot go faster than a walk, after the first morning spurt the team makes. The horse that Marion had caught to ride that morning was not a bronc, but was a beautiful silver-grey pony, branded Figure 8 on both hips. He was what they called a "spoilt horse," or outlaw, was six or seven years old, and had such a bad name that the boss put him in McGinty's mount. This horse weighed about 950 pounds, was as fat as mud, pretty as a picture, and had no saddle marks on his back—a bad sign for the rider. By careful and expert work, Marion got him away from the remuda without letting him pitch, and we started back to hunt the lost horses. However, when Dynamite, as they called him, saw that the saddle horses were trotting up the road in the other direction, he commenced to look back and prance around, stamping his feet and feeling with his mouth, to see if he could get that head where he wanted it.

By this time we had got about a mile from the wagon, and Marion, seeing the horse would not be satisfied until he got his pitch out, pulled him up and said, "Damn you, I will just see if I can ride you." Getting down, he took the hobble rope off the horse's neck and tied the stirrups together loosely under his belly. Swinging back into the saddle, he gave Dynamite free rein and struck him lightly with both spurs right behind the front cinch. At the first jump after McGinty hit the saddle, this pony put on the wicked fence-row twist, and for seventy-five yards he went like a cyclone. Springing high in the air, he would throw his head between his forelegs and give a twist in his back, so that it looked like he was bound to hit the ground on his head, but every time he would light on his feet, crouch like a wild cat, and leap as far and as high as he could, each time turning his other side to the sun as he came down. At about seventy-five yards, he whirled in the air and came pitching like mad, back towards me. It looked like no mortal man could stay on a horse like that without "clawing leather," but the man was still on him, sitting firmly in the saddle, when the horse quit pitching. If McGinty ever touched the saddle horn, I never saw it.

We talked a little bit, and Marion said, "I don't think he has got enough yet." Then reaching down, he slapped the horse on the shoulder with his left hand. Of course this made him call for his rider again, but as he was just a little bit winded by this time it was not so hard for the bronc peeler to set on him. As Dynamite pitched back by where I sat on my horse, I saw the boy take the bridle reins and the saddle horn in one hand, and reach way down on his forelegs, slapping him on the ankles and grabbing at his fetlocks as he pitched; then changing the bridle reins to the other hand, he reached down the other foreleg and slapped him on the ankles again. To wind up the ride, he reached back in the pony's flanks and grabbed a hand full of the soft skin there, pulling it up, first on one side and then the other, until the pony quit pitching. When he trotted up to where I was still sitting on my horse, Dynamite's nostrils were spread wide apart, his sides were heaving, his silver coat was wet with sweat, and water dripped off his fetlocks to the ground. His head was still carried proud, but the fire of battle had died out of his eyes and he seemed to say, in horse language, "I did my best to throw you, now I am ready to quit." Marion was breathing pretty hard himself, but he had the little dancing Irish light in his eyes that always showed when he pulled some daredevil stunt.

He looked over at me, grinned, and said, "I guess we had better go on now, and find those horses." If Dynamite ever threw McGinty off after that ride, I never heard of it. This pony was not cut up with the spurs, or damaged in any way, but he was pretty well tamed and did not pitch very much after that time. Marion had twelve or fifteen young broncs, from three to five years old, in his mount. They nearly all pitched a good deal for about a month, but I never saw him tie up his stirrups after he rode Dynamite that morning. He was not thrown and he did not cripple a horse that summer.

There was a four year old light bay horse in his mount, named Dime, that Marion said could pitch nearly as hard as Dynamite. He was a fast, wicked jumper, and went high in the air, but I never saw him put the extra twists in his show like the silver-grey outlaw. Nearly every man that worked on the range in that territory had from two to eight horses in his mount that would pitch if anything went wrong, but most of them were called "broke" horses, and some were good cow horses. Many a cool morning a well-trained cow horse would go off with a hump in his back, and if the rider did not hold that head up carefully, he would suddenly throw it down between his forelegs and pitch for fifty yards, either because he felt good, or did not feel good, or because the rider had kicked him in the stomach while putting the saddle on him that day or for some other good reason that he never mentioned.

Many of these horses were slightly "locoed"; that is, they had eaten some loco weed, which grew in valleys over the country. This weed would ruin a horse's temper, make him think every stick lying on the ground was a snake, every kick in the stomach was an insult, even though it was merely given to make him stand still. Finally, after a horse had eaten too much, it would drive him raving crazy so that he would eat nothing else, get poor, stagger around, and have fits until death came to end his suffering.

Most of the men could ride pretty well, and if a puncher kicked his horse in the stomach to make him stand still, while the saddle was put on his back, he usually knew what he would get when he crawled up into the saddle. I have seen this tried lots of times, and with the old cow horses on the gyp water ranges, it always made them mad and caused trouble. Just before we started up to the 8 Ranch that spring, I got the hardest fall of my life. It was off a six-year-old Z Bar roan horse that belonged to Mr. Lanier. He had not pitched in three years, and I had no quarrel with the horse, neither did I kick him in the stomach, but when I saddled him up and started to ride off, not thinking of any trouble, he suddenly downed his head and jumped so high I could plainly see the inside of a wagon bed standing near. I lit on his neck that time, and the next jump he flung me to the ground with such force that it laid me up for two days. Probably this horse had eaten too much of the loco weed. Many of the gentle ponies would after eating loco wake up and throw these fits sometimes when least expected. On this account, it soon became second-nature for me to watch the whites of their eyes when getting on the gentlest of those old range cow ponies.

Chapter IV

Breaking in a Green Stray Man

∿∿

MY FIRST COW WORK was somewhere in the cedar brakes north of the 8 Ranch. I think it was on the Wichitas—three big creeks, or small rivers, known as the North, Middle, and South Wichita rivers. Each prong usually ran a small stream of salt and gyp water from springs in the canyons, but it was unfit for human use. There was a good deal of rough country in here. We made a drive one day and camped for dinner where the roundup was thrown together in a small valley, called Yamperika Canyon.

While riding wildly that morning through the scrub oak, or "shinnery," that covered the hills, trying to keep up with the drive, I was astonished to see some wild cattle dash into scrub oak and one old fierce-looking brown cow crawl into a clump of brush and lie down, just as a panther or wild cat would do. The outlaw cattle were on the side of a hill, slightly to one side from the direction I was going, and when I galloped towards them, ten or fifteen head broke from the thicket and tore off through the hills, their white horns flashing in the sun and the white bush of their tails flying in the air, as they leaped swiftly over the rocky ground. I made no attempt to head them, as men scattered along that side of the drive ahead of me knew much better than I did how to handle them.

Two or three head tied down near the roundup ground that morning tried to run off from the herd.

As I knew nothing about this work, I watched the other boys as intently as a bird dog points quail. It looked to me at first as if half the men would get killed before they got all the cattle together in the roundup. No one got hurt, but I laid awake that night and wondered how a bunch of men could ride so reckless without the horses falling on them and killing them on the lime rocks. After watching Mr. Arnett and two or three other men ride in the herd and cut the round-up, I began to understand what they were after. The "cut" was "held"; that is, all the brands any of the men wanted were cut out and kept in charge of two or three punchers, the rest of the cattle each day, after the herd was "trimmed," or "worked," being turned loose on the range. In this way we got together in the next few days quite a number of cattle. These were called the "day herd," and from the first roundup on, herders stayed with this day herd constantly, grazing them by day and driving them from one roundup ground to the next, and at night guarding them in relays. These cattle were grazed or moved near the wagon by day, and were kept about two or three hundred yards from the camp at night.

In a week or ten days, the men were all known to me by their real names or their nicknames. Some of them were never known by their real names. Being a greenhorn, I asked two or three of the most reckless boys how they kept from killing themselves on the rocks. "Tige" Sloan told me that was the way to do, that it was better to run a horse full speed over the rocks than to try to pull him around, as the horse was not so apt to fall in rough country when he could manage himself as he was if the man tried to guide him. Will Lanier and all the other reckless young punchers said about the same, and they said the cedar brakes were not near as dangerous to ride in as the flat, open prairies where the prairie dogs had their holes. The little fellows were not killed out then like they are now, and the prairies in lots of places were full of them. They dig deep holes to live in, and bank the dirt up around them to keep the water out when it rains. Then the industrious animals dig numberless little shallow holes, about the size of a horse's foot, at the top of the ground, which they use to hide in if a hawk swoops down. Grass roots are their main food.

The littles holes are the ones the horses step in. No horse used to a dog town country will step in a big dog hole, but the little ones, sometimes covered with grass, are the ones that are dangerous. I have often seen a wild cowboy chasing a speedy cow or calf across the flat go down in a cloud of dust. When the horse steps in a "pup hole" at full speed, his head goes to the ground first, the rider is shot out of the saddle next, and the horse turns a somersault next and hits the ground on top of the saddle tree, with all four feet in the air. If the rider is lucky, he falls far in front of the horse and does not get hurt.

While the outfit was working through this rough country, three stray men came to the wagon with mounts of horses, their beds packed on one of them. They worked for ranches lying in the country we were in, and when the 8's got as far north as Crowell in Foard County, they cut their cattle out of our herd and went back home. These stray men were Jim

Williams, who worked for the Lightning Stripe outfit, a long stripe running down the shoulder of the cow; Jim Stout, a stuttering cowpuncher; and Shug Reynolds, a heavy, dark-skinned man, about thirty-two years old, who had been a bronc peeler, like McGinty, but had been promoted and was drawing top wages for the 3D outfit. I never knew who owned this brand, but don't think it belonged to any of the Waggoners, as they were way over to the north and east of this territory. Reynolds was a jolly, good-natured man; he could tell lots of funny tales around the camp, and he was also an expert cowhand and rider, though very reckless with a rope.

I was coming to camp at noon one day, the other men having had dinner and relieved me, as they had to finish working the cattle. The wrang was still holding the horses at the wagon for two other men and myself to catch our mounts. Jim Stout and Shug Reynolds were catching theirs. I was on a horse called Box, a heavy-set bay, a fast smooth runner. As we topped a small hill near the wagon, a wild looking bay horse left the remuda in a cloud of dust. Anxious to do something, I set out to try to bring him back, as there was no one on horseback at the remuda except the wrang. When I put the spurs to old Box, he gladly took after the horse, and soon we gained on him enough to see he had a long catch rope, or lariat, around his neck, with one end trailing behind him on the ground. We chased him at full speed for a half or three-quarters of a mile, when old Box went past him like a spirit, and circled the horse back into the remuda, with very little help from me, and no damage done except that my shirt sleeves were torn in a few places by the brush.

Riding up, I could hear some deep groans coming from under the chuck wagon, and Jim Stout, the stuttering cowboy, told me that "S-S-Shug R-R-Reynolds c-c-caught one of those big 3D horses on horseback, and the horse l-l-left the r-r-remuda, like a b-b-bat out of h-h-hell, jerked Shug's horse flat on his side, snapped the rope in two at the saddle horn, and went t-t-to the t-t-tulies." The stuttering man added, "I got on my h-h-horse to go after h-h-him, but when I s-s-seen the t-t-tracks y-y-your horse made across t-t-that sandy place, I knew it w-w-was no use to go." They spread Reynolds's bed out under the wagon and dragged him into it. As the outfit did not move until the next morning, Shug got up then and rode, although he was a little sore for a couple of days from the fall.

The first roundup the 8 wagon made west of Crowell was on a fine open prairie, near a little store and post-office called Vivian, in Foard County. As six or eight more stray men had come to the outfit by this time, bringing seventy-five or eighty fresh horses that had not been ridden much, a good many horses were bucking and pitching around with their saddles, and some with their riders, when they started to go on this drive. No one got thrown, and after the ponies all had their little "spells" to work off their surplus energy, the boss struck a lope and, making a big circle, he dropped off one or two of us at a time, going around all the cattle in sight. They were all started back towards the wagon, and then the roundup was thrown together near the little store on the prairie.

Being new at the game, I did not get back to the herd until the cutting had already started. Mr. Arnett and Will Lanier were cutting cattle on the side of the herd next to me, and two of the stray men were cutting their cattle on the other side of the herd into another cut. There were lots of cattle in that roundup. The 8 boss was riding Old Hub, his pet cutting horse. Hub was usually tied near the wagon, and when the drive came in, Mr. Arnett would lope down and saddle him up to work the herd. Hub was then about eight or nine years old, a fine looking bay, with a regal step and a beautiful head. He was the top cow horse of the 8 Ranch. I've written some more about him in the last chapter of this book.

They had cut twenty-five or thirty head out when I rode up to the herd. A Figure 8 man, Tom Davidson, was watching the herd on my right when old Hub brought out a wild red cow close to me. She had no calf and came out running sideways, wringing her tail and looking back at the horse, watching for a chance to dodge him and get back in the herd. After a couple of quick dodges, the wild cow, finding the bay horse looking her right in the face each time, whirled to run and tore out across the flat. As she did this, old Hub turned like he knew that job was done, and fox-trotted back into the herd. Hearing an exclamation from Tom Davidson on my right, I turned to see him bent low over his horse's mane, dashing madly after the wild cow. She had passed by the cut, dodging the man who tried to throw her into it, and was kicking up spurts of dust on her way to the hills.

Tom was riding a dark bay Figure 8 horse with a long black mane and tail, and I could see Tom was taking his rope down, for the loop floated plainly in the air behind him. When he ran up by her side, the cow threw down her head and charged at him full speed. His horse swung to one side, and as she passed by, the cowboy spun the loop with marvelous speed around his head, and, making a loose and careless cast, as it seemed to my untrained eyes, threw the loop over both horns. Then, jerking the rope, Tom threw the slack over the cow's back, and when the horse hit the end of the rope, she fell on her side. The puncher jerked his hobble rope off his horse's neck, tied her down, took his rope off her horns, and came trotting back to the roundup. This was the first time I had ever actually seen a wild brute tied down at a roundup, and while that was a half century ago, before rodeo work became known, it has never been my lot to see in any arena any better work than Tom Davidson did that morning.

While helping to hold that roundup together, I got my first hard fall. It was caused by my horse's stepping in one of the pup holes on the prairie. This horse was a limber-necked chestnut sorrel, branded HL connected on the left hip. He was pretty fast, but had no cow sense and was a "moon hunter"; that is, a horse that throws his head up in the air while running, instead of keeping it level with his body and watching the ground. We were lined up with a wild cow that had run off from the herd, and I was trying to do like Tom Davidson did with his cow, only I was not trying to rope her when the sorrel stepped in a small dog hole. It seemed to me that he scooted along on his nose for thirty feet before he turned over. When the end came, he stood almost upright on his head for a second and then fell right across me, with the saddle horn on one side and the cantle in the ground on the other side of my body. Flopping over on his side, the horse frantically waved his feet and legs over me till he got a toe hold, and then got up without stepping on my prostrate form.

At this same roundup one of the men cutting cattle on the other side of the herd flew into a rage and beat his horse over the head with his rope. This looked cruel, but we had mighty little of this kind of thing. Most of the men rode good horses and treated them well.

The boss had given me first choice of my time to stand night guard, and Cap Weatherly advised me to go on with him. He had first guard and said it was the easiest guard there was, because we could go to bed and sleep all night after coming off duty, unless a storm came up. We would have to pay for this privilege, however, he said, by remaining ignorant, "because we could not hear all the smart talk that went on around the fire after supper." I stayed on first guard with Cap until they started back to the 8 Ranch with the first herd.

The young men did not like to be put on day herd, because they would miss going on the drive that day, and it was lots more fun to go on the drive, do lots of running and rope the wild cattle than it was to lay around and take care of the day herd. I remember one day when me and "Tige" Sloan were on day herd together, we got busy and castrated two little two-year-old bulls that were prowling around near the cattle. They were both sorry specimens, and we kept running them off, and they kept coming back until Tige got mad and ran one out across the flat, caught and tied him down. By the time we got through with him, the other one had come back into the herd; so we tended to him too.

The second bull being a size or two larger than the first one, Tige caught him by the horns and told me to rope him by the heels. It was time for me to learn to rope cattle, he said, if I wanted to work with that outfit and make a good hand. Nothing could have suited me better; so, galloping past the animal, which was now plunging and leaping in the air on the end of Tige's rope, I made a lucky throw and caught both the little bull's heels in my loop. He decided to leave about the time my rope tightened on his hind feet and nearly jerked my horse from under me. This was because I did not know how to handle my horse. After a good deal of clawing and scratching on my part, I got back in the saddle before the horse thought about it, and he tried to throw me off. While clinging to the saddle horn, I made up my mind right there never to let another bull, even a two year old, get a run off to one side from my horse again. When a roped brute runs off to one side from a horse, the jerk is liable to jerk the horse from under you, or it will jerk him around with his head to it. If the animal is heavy and is running fast, it will sometimes jerk the horse flat on his side. On the other hand, if the animal pulls straight behind a horse or straight out in front, there is no danger.

Chapter V

Bulls of Earth and Sky

IF WE GOT THROUGH with the morning drive in time, the boss would make another drive after dinner and thus work two roundups a day. If it was desirable to move camp, he would take the wagon and horses on and hunt another camp, leaving the day herd to come on behind. A good boss would always go, or send a man, ahead when working a range that the outfit had never been over. This man would scout out a camp convenient to grass and enough water for men and horses. He tried to locate holes of fresh rainwater in creeks, as all the permanent water in that country came from gyp water springs in the hills and the salt water in the rivers. The day herd had to do without water until the outfit came to a creek with large pools of gyp water or to a river. Then the cattle would be moved down in the valley and grazed until they watered out good.

At the time and in the locality of which I write, Hereford cattle had not yet taken the outside range. Ranchers had commenced to breed them in the big pastures, but practically all of the outside, open range cattle, from the Double Mountain River on the south to Red River on the north, were a cross between native Longhorns with Durham or Devon blood. None of these cattle showed any Mexican strain. They were, especially the wild cattle, all large, power-ful brutes, totally unlike the magazine pictures of the

thin, scrawny specimens supposed to be the early in-
habitants of the Texas ranges. There were lots of big
red, wrinkled-necked bulls in those brakes, and while
none of the boys knew their ancestry, no one could
say the bulls did not know how to take care of themselves. When one of these old, wild, red bulls turned
his bloodshot eyes in my direction, it was easy for me
to ride off to a safe distance.

A calf resulting from a cross between one of these
big bulls on a native-born Pease River cow that never
had seen a wire fence might be a red, or red-and-
white spotted, or even a sulphur colored, yellow animal, but he always contained more dynamite, more
actual speed, and more weight on the end of a rope
than any breed of cattle known to me then or later.
While there was lots of fine grass, both curly mesquite
and needle grass, in that country, I have an idea that
the scalawags all died or were killed. In the winter,
the cattle had the ever present danger of quicksand
in the river, where they all had to water when the
creeks dried up in the hills. In the spring, the big grey
lobos were bad to eat the yearlings and weak cattle
wandering off by themselves back up in the hills in
search of fresh grass. Nature operated in those days
according to the old law of the survival of the fittest.
Cattle, horses, and also men who were not physically
fit and healthy soon died or disappeared.

There was lots of rain in that spring of 1894, most
of it coming up at night; consequently, it did not
bother much, except for the loss of sleep, as the days
were usually fair enough to keep on working. One of
the worst storms in my recollection came up one night

while the outfit was camped on some open hilly country in the upper part of the 9 range, northwest of Crowell and south of Pease River. The regular guard was two men, and Cap Weatherly and I were standing first guard, but the ground was wet and the cattle did not want to lie down; so the boss added an extra man to each guard that night. George Thompson was the third man on our guard when we took the herd. It was nearly dark when the day men went to the wagon; there was not a breath of wind, the air seemed oppressive, and a big cloud was slowly approaching from the northwest.

To add to our troubles, a big bull came up from the outside bent on having battle with five or six range bulls in the herd. We tried to whip him off with ropes, but he was not afraid of a man on horseback. When we chased him, he would stop and bow that neck and walk back to meet us. There was nothing to do but to either let him come in the herd and have his fight or shoot him. We let him come. His bawling and bellering called up another bull still bigger, and he got into the herd also. After pawing up the ground and giving tongue to their blood-curdling roars for five or ten minutes, they soon started a couple of fights. In the gathering darkness, we heard the deadly crack of their horns as they charged each other in furious combat. Cap Weatherly told me when the bulls got in the herd they would fight. "Now, kid," he said, "when those bulls fight all they want to, the one that gets whipped is coming out of that herd, and you be damn sure to keep out of his way, for a fighting bull is the fastest thing on earth on four feet, for a short run. One of those bulls will kill your horse and you too, if you happen not to get out of their way when they come out."

We were all three riding around the herd in opposite ways, trying to keep the cattle together. Suddenly there was a furious crash, a roar of pain, and a huge bull broke out of the herd, followed by his opponent, both charging like mad. The victor hooked his adversary every jump till he left the herd. Then he stopped and, pawing up the ground with his forefeet, soon recovered his breath. As he came stalking back through the darkness to the cattle, he was giving deep bellows from the bottom of his mighty chest. In a few minutes one of the other two combatants got whipped and vanished into the black night on the south side of the herd. The fighting stirred up the cattle, but riding at a lope in different directions around them, we soon got them quiet after the bull fights were over.

It was now about ten o'clock. Still there was no wind, though the coming storm was in plain view, its mighty crest piled high with black rolling clouds and the lightning coming straight to the ground. To the eyes of a tenderfoot kid the night looked like it would be the last night of the human world. We all wore good slickers and the fear of getting wet did not bother me like the looks of that cloud. The blackness, the steady roar of wind and rain advancing with relentless speed behind what looked like a solid curtain of water approaching us across the hills, and the furious claps of thunder, all scared me bad for a while. Suddenly a blinding flash of pure white light blazed in my face; a streak of liquid fire hit the prairie just across the herd from me with a fierce metallic crack that jarred the ground under my horse's feet; a crash of thunder burst overhead that sounded as if the end of time had come, while the quick, thudding sound of hoof-beats told me the cattle were leaving the bed ground. In a second, the rain was falling in sheets, while flash after flash of lightning blazed overhead, and many bolts of the white fire struck the hills around us.

Dazed and breathless, I could hardly sit on my horse. But, unknown to me at the instant, my two companions were, in the fury of the storm, riding at breakneck speed around the herd, one behind the other, in order to get to the lead cattle. When Mr. Arnett came from the wagon at the head of the riders, I was across the herd. At sight of him dashing through the white glare of the lightning, down the other side of the moving cattle, all my courage came back to me. I realized that his sturdy honest spirit knew no fear. Galloping quickly around the back end of the cattle, I "burnt the breeze," as Cap Weatherly used to say, trying to catch up with the wild riding cowboys and help hold the herd.

The forward riders soon turned the leaders, and swung the whole herd around in a long loop, the leaders coming back through the tail end of the cattle. But they broke through and ran for a ways down in the valley about a mile south of camp, where the boys checked them again. Here the cattle started to "milling around" some. After that the frightened cattle would drift with the rain until a fresh burst of the storm would start them running again. Then when

lightning lit up the earth I could see galloping horsemen in the lead of the cattle, slowing them up gradually and swinging them around to walk in a circle.
For hours they alternately drifted, ran, checked and
milled. Always when the cattle began running with
the storm, the men would ride to the front of them
from one side only. If seven or eight men on good
horses will run up to the point on one side only of a
stampeded herd, it is usually easy to outrun them and
circle the leaders back into the tail cattle, and the
whole herd will then usually go to milling. If riders
rush up to the running leaders—the point of a herd—
on both sides, they will find it is hard to outrun them
and very likely won't do anything but split the running cattle up without stopping them. Some bosses
don't want but a man or two to help put a stampede
into a mill. In a pitch black night a whole outfit of
riders may add to confusion instead of bringing order.
That night in the almost constant lightning, I could
see the dark forms of the running horses and the
yellow slickers of the lead men as they turned the
running cattle on the side of a hill, while the other
men came on after them, all cooperating to wind the
panic-stricken cattle into a ball.

I sure was glad when that rain began to slack up
and George Thompson galloped up, with the water
still running off his hat and slicker, and told me the
other guard had them. Although we did not stay out
there all night, it seemed to me it had been a mighty
long time since the sun went down. My horse on this
trip was a tall, dark-colored dun, with an iron gray
mane and tail; he had been a hard-pitching horse in

his youth, and while he never pitched with me, he was a strong, determined old veteran who never fell down or stepped in a dog hole as long as he was in my mount. The boss did not move camp the next day, and we all spread our bedding out on the grass and dried it out good. Cal Lowry found a lot of wild mulberries on a little rocky hill near camp, and made a big mulberry cobbler for supper. Cap and I nearly had another run on our guard that night after eating part of that cobbler. The good supper made us sleepy, and near the end of our guard one of us struck a match to see what time it was. The sudden light made both horses jump, and the cattle jumped too, but we quickly rode around them and they did not do anything.

About two days after the big rain, we reached Pease River with the herd and camped for dinner in a little valley against the river bank. Stretching back from the bluff where the road crossed the river, this open grassy valley contained about 200 acres. In it stood an old house, sheltered from the blizzards of winter by the red bluffs and cedar to the north. To the south, Catfish Creek emptied into the river, and another bluff set in below the mouth of "Cat," overlooking the red waters of the old Pease running far to the sunrise. This was one of the most used crossings on the river, and was well known by all the different outfits that worked in that country.

Chapter VI

It's Now We've Crossed Pease River

WHILE WE ATE our noonday meal in that little valley above the mouth of Catfish Creek, the herd, in charge of two day herders, grazing near the wagon, a lively conversation went on as to whether the river was swimming. None of us except two or three of the boys who lived in that part of the country knew any-think about the crossing. Knowing there was only one man who could tell us anything, some of the boys asked the boss, who was sitting cross-legged on the ground eating his dinner, if he was going to cross the herd. Mr. Arnett said, "Yes, I want to put the herd across right after noon, as the river might rise in a couple of hours so we could not tackle it. I believe it is fordable for the wagon now."

After dinner most of the boys privately decided to catch their best swimming horses, as the water might be deeper than the boss thought. Before we mounted to move the cattle up to the crossing, each man rigged himself up for swimming. Most of the men tied their boots, spurs and gloves on their saddles, while some of the younger boys took off all their clothes except boots and hats. They figured that if they got into a tight, they could kick their boots off in the water and swim out. There were about 1500 head of cattle in the herd besides the calves.

There was a large brown, motley-faced steer with the biggest set of horns on his head that he could grow. For some reason unknown to me, this old steer was fairly gentle. Every day when we started the cattle to moving he always got up and took his self-appointed position as leader of the herd. I do not remember his brand or who owned him, but they were taking him back to the prairie country north of the river. Perhaps as a work ox he had been lost from some emigrant train or buffalo wagons crossing the country in an early day. Whatever his occupation had been, he was a born leader. Now as we headed the cattle up the road and into the river, the big ox, as usual, placed himself at the lead. He showed no fear when he got to the edge of the water. He put his head down as if to look at the road and walked off into that dark, swift, treacherous-looking water as calmly as a man seining for minnows will wade into a clear, shallow creek.

Seeing that their old leader thought there was no danger, the cows followed, dry cattle first, the cows with calves bringing up the rear. This was one of the finest sights in my experience that summer, to see the whole herd in the river, strung out to a thin line in front, the leaders walking out on the far side while the last of the drag cows and calves went into the water. The water did not swim our horses more than fifteen or twenty steps out in the middle of the river, though it was deep enough to swim most of the cattle for a good ways, and even the big lead steer was drifted down the stream twenty-five or thirty yards when he reached the swift current and the quicksand in the middle of the river. We had a good laugh at the boys who had pulled off all their clothes, though their garments tied on behind the saddles did not get wet like ours when the horses struggled through the quicksand. Will Lanier crossed with nothing on but his hat and boots. A fine stalwart young man, over six feet tall and built like an athlete, with very fair skin and light hair, he made a striking picture as he rode into the red water on a big sorrel horse. Will was a top hand all right, equally good at crossing a boggy river in the quicksand or in swimming water, in a roundup, or working the wild cattle on a drive. He always worked with the lead cattle.

Finding the river too deep to cross the wagon without getting a lot of water in the wagon bed and damaging flour and other provisions, the boss told us to graze the cattle until mid-afternoon and then they would try crossing the wagon, as the river was going down pretty fast. As I was left with three or four men on the day herd and the cattle were still grazing near the river bank, I could see everything that went on. When they got ready to cross the wagon and the saddle horses, the four mules were hitched up, the cook mounted to his seat and took the lines, a man or two helped the wrangler move his horses into the crossing ahead of the wagon, and the rest of the men rode along by the wagon to "tie on" in case it needed help. A bluff six or eight feet high, where the road ran into the river, prevented the riders from tying their ropes onto the wagon before all were out in the water. Then, sure enough, the heavy loaded wagon stuck on the sandbar. A man quickly jumped off his horse on each side of the wagon and, wading up close, tied all the ropes to some part of the bed or running gear.

With three or four good stout cow horses pulling on these ropes tied to their saddle horns on each side of the wagon, they managed to "snake" the heavy load out of the water, although one or two of the mules fell down in the boggy places and one horse bogged down. The rider had to jump off and take his rope off the saddle horn before his horse could get up.

Although Pease River was not as large as the Double Mountain Fork or the Salt Fork of the Brazos or the Canadian River, I believe it was the most dangerous river to cross in Texas. The banks were always bad on one side or both, and it was so hard to get out of, once you got in, that most people stayed out until they knew it was not swimming. After crossing Pease River, the outfit commenced to work the prairie, north to the Denver Railroad as far west as Childress.

On the edge of the open country north of the river, there lived a man named Jobe Brazile, with his wife and two little children and his nephew Tobe Brazile, a lad about fifteen years old. Mr. Brazile was looking after all the cattle that had been moved up there from Stonewall County the year before, and he also had a job with the 8 outfit and rode a mount of Figure 8 horses. I was sent to Mr. Brazile with instruction to place myself at his command. After I reached his place, he gave me the "powders" from then on until we got through work that fall. When we had worked as far north as the Denver Railroad, at a point between Childress and Quanah, Mr. Arnett had to leave, and he turned the outfit over to Jobe Brazile for a few days.

About the first thing that happened after Mr. Brazile took charge was another big rain and stampede. The herd had been driven up near the Denver Railroad, quite a lot more cattle had been gathered, and one evening the new boss moved the whole outfit over north across the railroad track about a mile to camp. The track was not fenced then, and all this country between Pease and Red rivers was a wide open prairie, with just a few small pastures fenced here and there where people had settled. Having hobbled the horses for the night, between the herd and the railroad, we bedded the cattle down as usual, and after supper Cap Weatherly and myself went on guard. Nothing happened on our guard, though it got awful dark and cloudy, but sometime in the night a big rain came up from the north, and everybody had to get up and go to the herd.

We had about 2500 head of cattle, counting the stray men's stock and the Figure 8's, in the herd. My night horse that night was a tall bay that Mr. Brazile had put in my mount. He was branded a Roman cross on the left shoulder, and he was no account for a night horse, or anything else, because he got scared at everything he saw in the dark. I don't think this horse had ever been out at night with any one on him. He would jump and snort every time the lightning flashed, instead of watching the cattle like my other night horse did. A good night horse will watch the cattle and run when he sees them running, lots of times before the rider sees them leave the herd. The cattle did not run very far, and we milled them around before they got across the railroad and held them a while.

That was the darkest night of all my experience in guard duty that summer. The clouds seemed to come close to the ground and cover us with inky darkness. There was a good deal of electricity, and the weird, uncanny balls of fire played on the ears of my horse and on the horns of the cattle with a pale, unearthly blue-white flame. The little balls would appear and disappear in the pitch black night and it was not hard to imagine they were the lights from the other world, shining in long-dead eyes of ghosts that had come to earth to sport themselves in mockery on the backs of a phantom herd. Everything seemed unreal that night. Even the cattle looked like ghosts. On account of there not being much bad lightning, I guess the little fires playing around all over the herd looked more spooky than they would have looked under sheet lightning. The cattle did not run much but they drifted all night, and when morning came I was still with the main part of the herd. Sometime during the rain the cattle had split into two bunches, ours being still near the wagon. The others were south of the track, five or six miles from camp, but part of the men had stayed with them, and they brought them back the next morning.

To add to our misery, the rain had drifted the horses across the railroad, and a train had come along and stampeded them too. It took all the next day to get the herd together and move it farther away from the track. Our new boss made two mistakes here: he held the herd too close to the railroad, and he turned the hobbled horses out too close to the track. One might think that anybody could be a good wagon boss, but it takes lots of foresight to run a bunch of men and look after all the matters that come up with a good sized cow outfit.

A reader used to the accounts given by many writers of the large herds that were handled in Texas in an early day may think it queer that we did not have over 2500 or 3000 head of cattle together at any one time that summer. Three thousand was the limit, and the outfit never gathered over 2000 head, generally fewer, in any one day's roundup. The character of the country, the wild nature of the cattle, and the fact that we held only those cattle in brands represented by the Figure 8 wagon accounted for the limited size of our herd. While there was a good deal of open prairie land between the forks of the Wichita River and the breaks on Pease River, and again between Pease River and Red River, still most of the range we worked in was broken country. In a country like this, cut up with deep canyons, one right after the other, running back from the river on both sides, it was impossible to throw a large roundup together. If there had been fifty men with the wagon, they could not have gathered three thousand cattle in any one roundup out of the cedar-brake hills, because the cattle were too wild, and there were too many places for them to quit the drive and get away. While working in the rough country, the boss usually made short drives, and made two roundups each day.

Chapter VII

Horse Stampede

THE SECOND DAY after the big rain and stampede, the herd was moved west, towards Childress, for ten or twelve miles, and I was detailed to help the horse wrangler move the horses. We were told to drive the horses right up the railroad track a few miles and then cross over and take them to the wagon, which would be camped for dinner a mile or so south of the railroad. It was a bright sunshiny morning after the rain, grass was fine, the horses were trotting along on the north side of the Denver tracks, when we came to where someone had fenced off a section of land next to the railroad, leaving a narrow lane between the fence on one side and the railroad tracks on the other. The lane ran for a mile ahead.

George Ratliff (the wrang) and I were riding along contentedly, talking about cowboy life and how easy the work was sometimes, when George suddenly glanced around and said, "Look yonder, behind us!" I looked and saw a big black engine, pulling a string of freight cars, about half a mile or so behind us rocking along right up the track. George charged the horses, trying to beat the train to the end of the lane, but they did not need any charging when they saw that engine coming. They left the ground and flew part of the time. George's horse was pawing them on their backs to get them out of the way, while mine was running almost crazed with fright, trying to keep up with the mad rush. We did our best, but the engine came out neck and neck with us at the end of the lane. The engineer and fireman were both looking out the cab window grinning at us. For a wonder, not a single horse jumped the fence. They just ran straight ahead. This was the second time they had been stampeded by a train. If the engineer had blown his whistle, it would have put every horse through the fence, but as it was, not one animal or man got hurt.

They spread out like a fan when they reached the end of that lane, but as that was all a wide open prairie, not a bush in the way, we soon had them rounded up, and gladly drove our horses away from that track on down to the wagon, which we could see camped ahead of us in a big valley, two or three miles south of the railroad. Of the 250 head of horses not a single one had got killed or even crippled in the wild get-away.

That night we camped close to Childress, and all the men went into town and saw some of the sights of civilization. There were churches and meeting-places under arbors roofed with bear-grass or made out of lumber, in all the little Texas towns of that period, and also saloons and gambling rooms and houses of prostitution. There was not much attempt to hide anything in those days and people openly lived the lives they chose. If they wanted to drink, they walked into the saloon and got whatever they wanted; if they wanted to pray, they went to church and got down on their knees and asked the Good Lord to forgive their sins; if two parties had trouble that could not be settled, they both got their guns and shot it out, in plain daylight. There were not so many cowardly murders then, because any man could carry a gun.

The next morning the wagon was taken to town and the boss bought a full supply of flour, coffee, beans, bacon, and syrup for a bunch of hungry men. The Figure 8 wagon always killed their own beef while working and had plenty of it. They would kill a six- or eight-months-old sucking heifer calf, and there was a good demand for that kind of beef three times a day. In a high, dry climate meat can be kept for several days by wrapping it up in a tarp, or slicker, putting it in the wagon in the day time and hanging it out at night.

Cal Lowry, the cook, was a famous hand to dress a fat calf, and he could cook a "cowboy stew" (or son-of-a-gun) to a queen's taste. After loading the chuck wagon and eating dinner that day, the outfit started back to the southeast. We worked a couple of days rounding up and gathering cattle before we camped on a little creek called Groesbeck, where Mr. Arnett rejoined us.

While at this place, a man came to the outfit from the Matador Ranch to look through the herd and get any cattle that we might have gathered for that company. I cannot remember his name, but this man was one of the most typical-looking "peelers" imaginable. Short and heavy-set, about forty years old, with a reddish brown mustache, brown hair and piercing eyes, he had every mark of the top hand. All his horses were good, and five or six of them were big, old Roman-nosed, hog-backed bays and red roans, that showed lots of white in their eyes. And when this old peeler mounted one, we would get to see a real show, for he would sit there calmly, without trying to pull his horse's head up, and strike him with the spur occasionally while the big horse (all his horses were fat as mud) would bawl and pitch around the camp to his heart's content. The boys that knew him said this man had had a bad fall with his horse, while working cattle several years back, and struck his head on a rock. He never knew anything until the doctors cut out a little three-cornered piece of his skull, where it was pressing down on the brain. Then the doctors placed a piece of pure silver of sufficient size to amply cover the space left open by the removed piece of skull and sewed the scalp carefully together over it. The boys said the silver plate was still in the man's head. Anyway, this man wore good clothes, rode the best Gallup saddle that was made, rode with two girts and no throat latch, and could sit on a pitching horse and watch him jump with all ease.

The outfit stayed at this camp for two or three days, and Mr. Arnett told all the stray men to cut their cattle first, as he intended to shape up the herd while here and take all the Figure 8 cattle back to the ranch in King County. By that time we had gathered about 1500 head of the 8 brand and there was 1000 head, maybe more, that belonged to the stray men. Before a herd was worked, it would be grazed for an hour or two after breakfast; then the stray men would catch their best cutting horses and the herd would be thrown together. Two of the stray men usually worked together if they lived near each other, cutting their cattle into the same bunch. Another man generally

held their cut, so that both men could work in the
herd at the same time. Two men can cut 150 to 200
head apiece, where they know the brands and ear-
marks, in about two hours.

It took most of the first day for the stray men to
get all their cattle out, and the next morning Will
Lanier and I cut the cattle we had in the herd and
took them to Mr. Brazile's place. That evening, the
Figure 8 outfit shaped up their herd, and the next
morning they started back to the King County ranch.
The two days' work gave us all a lot of "cutting" to
do, and I learned a whole lot, watching the other men
work and cutting some myself. My horse, partly
owing to my awkwardness, ran over a yearling while
I was trying to cut a cow and calf out of the roundup
and flattened the big calf out flat on the ground, but
the horse did not fall, though everybody said it was
"damned strange" the kid did not get killed. Once
Will Lanier sailed out across a dog town, riding a
fast, half-broken young bay horse called Streak, after
a wild calf that had left the herd. When his horse hit
a pup hole in the prairie, he turned "a cooler" in the
air and lit on his saddle horn, but Will got to his feet
laughing. Jumping on his bronc again, he made a fast
run and a good throw, bringing the calf back to the
roundup galloping on the end of his rope.

We had good times on that work, and I was sorry
to see the 8 wagon leave. They were all a good bunch
of men, and though Marion McGinty. George Ratliff,
Will Lanier, and Ross (Tige) Sloan, were the only
boys of my age in the outfit, all the men were kind to
me. They called me the Kid, because of my small size

and runty appearance, not because I was a top hand, like the famous Pitchfork Kid of those parts and certainly not because of any resemblance in disposition or looks to the terrible Billy the Kid of New Mexico. Many a night guard when the cattle were sleeping, and the moon shone almost like day, would Cap Weatherly turn his horse, while riding around the herd, and talk to me for half an hour or longer as we rode slowly around the cattle.

Good old Cap! He was the first one of the 8 men to take a lonely tenderfoot into his friendship, and I will never forget him. He was a typical puncher, dark-skinned, with raven black hair, a little under sized, but a top hand all around. He could mount a horse with more ease than most men, and he rode a beautiful, light bay horse in his mount called Whirlwind that the men said was a "tiger," but Cap had a way with horses and Whirlwind never even pitched with him. Cap told me afterwards that the next man that got this horse in his mount, after he quit work, was laid up for two weeks after Whirlwind threw him off. Cap Weatherly died with the yellow jaundice, long years ago. I never saw him but once after we worked together that summer. He was at the Cowboy's Reunion, at Haskell, Texas, in 1898, on his way to Irion County to take a job as cattle inspector, on the quarantine line down there. May his spirit be resting in peace, on the other side of the river, and may Cap always have a full share of all the blessings which come to those in "that land where no storm clouds rise." But it will not suit Cap unless they give him plenty of fat horses to ride, over the green ranges of Paradise.

Chapter VIII

Crossing Bad Water

ⱱⱱⱱ

WHEN MR. ARNETT headed the Figure 8 herd back to King County, he left a mount of horses for Mr. Brazile, and left Tommy Davidson with his mount, instructing them to work with every outfit that gathered cattle in that country. They were to gather all the Figure 8 cattle they could find and throw them back on some prairie country ten or twelve miles north of Brazile's place, where there was plenty of grass, with both creek and lake water. Will Lanier and I were throwing our cattle back on this prairie too, and as the 8's were coming back to work this locality in the fall, we expected to finish work with them.

Two wagons were working most of the time in this territory. One belonged to two brothers named Witherspoon, with headquarters close to Crowell, Texas. Their brand was Figure 9. It was on all their cattle, but they had two brands of stock horses in that range. One was a small device called a teaspoon on the left shoulder, and the other was L7 on the left hip. The Figure 9 wagon worked a big country, from the Wichitas on the south to Pease River on the north, for twenty or thirty miles up and down that river, and sometimes north to the Denver Railroad.

The other wagon belonged to White & Swearingen, and was known as the O X outfit, for they branded this brand in big letters on the right side. Their mark was under-bit each ear. Their range lay west of the 9 range, further up the river, and the O X wagon worked most of the country between Paducah and Crowell, north across both forks of Pease River to the Denver, west to the Matadors, and east to the 9 range.

Altogether there was a big lot of open country in there, and we worked up and down the river for fifty miles all that summer. At first it gave me the cold chills to ride up on the bank of that old river. There was so much rain that spring that it was always either up, or just fordable, but we had to cross it so much I got used to seeing the other men ride off into it, five or six in a bunch, and come out on a bar of quicksand that would shake like jelly under their horses' feet. However, quicksand is not dangerous unless the water is swimming. If a horse thinks he has struck bottom in swimming water and lets down in the quicksand, he is liable to go out of sight as well as his rider, for the sand will duck him unless he is a good river horse. Some horses learn the water and sand so well that they will take their time and get across most anywhere, while other horses get scared, and duck themselves and their riders every time they cross a boggy river.

Tommy Davidson was a hair-lipped man, and one of the best cowhands the 8's had on their payroll. He was of medium height, strong and powerful in body, but his affliction give him a stern, hard look that did not do him justice, as really he was a good companion, good-natured and honest. When we left the camp at Brazile's place after the 8 outfit went south, Tom and I took two mounts of horses and a bedroll and went down the river about twenty-five miles to see if the 9 wagon had gone to work. Finding that they were not at work, we started back to camp, intending to cross the river at the mouth of Catfish Creek.

There had been clouds up west of us and we expected the river to be up a little, but when we rode down to the river bank one hot afternoon about three o'clock, it did not look bad. The waves out in the center of the current were running fully two feet high, this was generally regarded as a sign that the river was not swimming. In these western rivers the quicksand is drifted by the swift current at a great rate. Now it is in the center, and again it is piled up on the sandbars along the sides, but high waves are always an indication of lots of quicksand. There are piles of it on the bottom of the channel and it will drift and roll under the water, making the surface of the water look as if the current were running over large rocks.

Getting off our horses, we reset the saddles and loosened the girts. No experienced puncher rides into deep water until the girts are loosened, so that the horse can draw plenty of air into his lungs and float part of the time while swimming, as most good river horses do. We did not then know this crossing very well, and carelessly got on our horses and drove the others off into the river.

I was on the lower side, and we had not got ten steps from the bank when all the horses floated off their feet and went to swimming across the red water. Tommy spurred in to help me keep them swimming straight. They were all good river horses, and every one of them swam straight out to the middle of the river. However, when they hit those high-rolling waves in the center of the current, it was too swift. The water splashed over them and scared them, turning the whole bunch downstream. We could not turn them back, as they shot past us in bunches. When the big waves hit them, our own horses had all they could do to stay on top and carry us. Seeing that my horse, a powerful, heavy-muscled sorrel, was far better than I in the water, I let him do what he thought best. Tom was about thirty feet down the river from me, and the eighteen saddle horses and Tom's pack horse were still farther down.

We could not see each other all the time as the red waves would roll up between us and almost let us down to the bottom sometimes. Thinking that the next wave would surely roll over my head, I would float up on a big swell and see Tom and the horses still fighting to get out of the swift current. All the time they were working towards the side we had come in on. Between a quarter and a half mile down the river from the crossing, was the mouth of Catfish Creek. All the horses were swimming for their lives and aiming to hit the river bank as high as they could above that creek. Soon the loose horses struck full force against the bank. Turning, they began to swim and work their way back up the river, hunting a place to crawl up the steep sides, about twenty feet high along here.

Tom was still ahead of me, and his horse was a little closer to the bank. Both our mounts were doing their best to follow the others, but having a saddle and a man each to carry, they could not swim as fast as the loose horses, and the current was rapidly driving them down stream. We knew if we went past the mouth of Catfish Creek, it was goodby, for a high red bluff set in below the creek and ran for a mile down the river on that side, and we knew the current would pin us both against that side until we drowned. No living thing could stem the tide if it carried us to the bend in the river. However, both our horses continued to fight and swim against that raging river with all their power. Then Tom's horse struck bottom on a ledge of red dirt on the upper side of this creek, and scrambled up the bank. My horse struck the same ledge and was knocked off of it by a big wave, but Old Spot knew that safety lay in the still water he could see in the mouth of that creek, and swimming furiously against that fatal tide, we suddenly shot into still water and safety. Swimming up the creek a short distance, the brave old horse found a trail and climbed up the bank to join our companion.

Tom Davidson had spent his life, after getting old enough to draw a man's wages, working on the bad waters of the Double Mountain River and the Salt Fork of the Brazos. He was a veteran of twelve or fifteen years spent with a roundup wagon in the summer and in a line-camp in the winter. He was in the prime of life, thirty-one or thirty-two years old. He was a cool and steady hand in any kind of trouble, but when we rode up on the bank together and looked back at that cliff below the mouth of Catfish and saw the boiling red water we had just got out of, seething and beating against that straight up-and-down wall of dirt far below us, I could see that his face was pale and his hand that held the bridle reins shook. Tom said, "Boy, we nearly went under that time." I said, "Yes. Even that little creek had the water backed up in it deep enough to swim a horse for fifty yards, and we did not think the river was swimming when we started to cross."

Turning, we started up the little valley to look for the horses. I was scared too bad to talk much for some time, and Tom was afraid his old favorite pack horse had drowned, as it did not seem possible that he could get out of the river, loaded as he was with a heavy bedroll, sufficient for two men to sleep in and it soaked with water besides. However, we had not ridden more than a quarter of a mile, when we saw the horses ahead of us, grazing near the old line camp, an old shanty that had been built for the boys to camp in when they rode the river to watch the "bog holes" in the winter and early spring. Tom was overjoyed to find Old Sugarfoot, as he called his pack horse, grazing with the others. The pack was still right side up, and the water was still dripping out of our bed.

After counting our horses, to see that none had been lost, we drove them into a little pen near the house, unpacked Sugarfoot and carried our dripping bed to the yard fence, where, after getting our extra underclothes, coats, pants, shaving outfit and Tom's tobacco out of the flour sacks we kept them in, we hung all the bedding on the fence to drain. Taking off our clothes, we wrung the water out of them and, putting our underclothes, socks and boots on, hung the rest of our garments on the fence. It being then about two hours till sundown, we staked our two night horses and hobbled the others out. Tom heaved a sigh of relief and said, "Right here is a good place to stay until that river goes down so we can see the sandbar on the other side." Tom rustled around for some grub in the cabin but there was not a thing to eat, and no matches. However, as my companion remarked, it was not near as hard to do without something to eat as it would have been to "lay dead on a sandbar down in that river somewhere, with the quicksand drifting over us!"

Although we had no idea the river was so deep, and had not caught any special swimming horses, it was the two horses that saved us. I will never forget them. Tom was riding a fine-looking dark brown Figure 8 horse, with a white star in his forehead, and my horse was a red sorrel, with a white star in his forehead and a white spot on his right hip, about three inches across. He was branded 47 on the left hip, and though he was about fifteen years old, Old Spot, as he was called, was strong and vigorous and knew more about deep water and quicksand than half the people, even in that country.

After camping in the cabin and enduring more or less patiently the discomfort of a rather damp bed, we went down bright and early the next morning and looked at the sticks we had stuck in the river bank at the edge of the water the night before. Finding the water had fallen three or four feet below our mark, we lost no time in getting our saddle horses together, taking their hobbles off, and packing the still damp bed on old Sugarfoot. We crossed at the ford in water about half-side deep to the horses, where it had been big swimming the evening before. As the pangs of hunger were becoming severe by this time, we hit a steady jog trot for camp. To feel the hard ground under the horses' feet was good. After a twenty-four hour fast, a scare that left me weak, a wetting that used up a lot of calories and a damp bed and no morning coffee, dinner that day was something to remember.

Chapter IX

Outlaws in the OX Breaks

THE NEXT DAY Tom Davidson took his mount and went to work with a wagon over north of Quanah and gathered some Figure 8 cattle that had strayed off over in that range. A day or two later Mr. Brazile and I took two mounts of horses and a pack outfit and went to work with the O X wagon. We found the outfit camped about ten miles south of Childress. There were a lot of big steers on their range, and the boss had orders to gather all they could get and ship them to market. They were so wild they were spoiling all the other cattle.

All this river range west of the forks of Pease River was called the O X Breaks. It was a rough, mean country to ride in. We crossed and recrossed the north and south forks of the river, making drives up and down them. Leaving the wagon where it could not be taken across the river, we would make the drive and work the roundup on the other side, bringing the cut back to the herd we were holding.

On this trip I had only six day horses and one night horse. Considering me a green hand, Mr. Brazile did not give me a full mount of horses, though most of them were smooth-running ponies. But they had been trained by right-handed ropers—and I was left-handed. When I took down my rope on one of them, he would do his best to run up on the left side of the cow brute. During the summer's work, it came my lot to ride three different mounts of horses, and there were only three ponies in the whole bunch that would willingly run up on the right side of a cow.

The O X wagon boss was a bad egg, and when we got to the outfit that first night, he was cursing with every other breath. A short, heavy, dark-skinned man, he was dressed carelessly in big hat, boots and spurs, and he acted and talked like a bad man from Bitter Creek. The cook and horse wrangler were both kids, harmless boys about eighteen or nineteen years old, and they were both hoodooed pretty bad. The other men did not have much to say, and the boss kept growling and cursing around the wagon all the time. I kept out of his way as much as possible, because he commenced to say a lot about damn kids, little brands, stray men who could not earn the grub it took to feed them. I expected to get cussed out or slapped over.

We had made only two or three roundups before this boss had some kind of an altercation with a fine-looking man from the Mill-Iron Ranch, Horace Wilson by name. He was a top hand and a fine man. He was riding with one boot in the chuck-wagon on account of a horse having fallen on him and mashed his foot. He hit the O X boss such a blow in the face with his fist that it broke three of the bones in the back of his hand and the O X company lost a wagon boss. Some of the men thought there would be a killing, but the boss sent to town for a livery team, packed up his bed and left as soon as the rig came out. Two or three of his teeth were knocked out. Horace Wilson's hand got so bad that he had to go back to the Mill-Iron Ranch, and they sent another man to work in his place.

The O X company put Sherman Swearingen, then a young man and a brother to one of the owners, in charge of the wagon. He moved it down on the river and commenced work again in the breaks. Sherman Swearingen and his brother Tom, who was also with the outfit, were exactly opposite in character, Sherman being a quick, lively, jocular young man, with light complexion and blue eyes, while Tom was a tall, dark young fellow, solemn most of the time and quiet as an owl.

Another O X hand was Ward Dwight, a small man not much bigger than myself, of dark, swarthy complexion, with a bad scar on the side of his neck, a wild and daring rider of the first rank; no man ever took any more chances; he stopped for nothing when a steer with a big set of horns left the drive and broke off through the cedars, and I never saw him miss a throw at a running brute. Other cowboys on that work represented the Pitchforks, Shoe Buckles, Matador, Nines, Ball and Twine and other brands. Among them were Pat Berry, Joe Ragsdale, Jim Thompson, a man named Estey or Estes, John Kiggin, Tinker Williams, and an old man every one called Bally; I never heard his name, but the boys all tried to keep away from him during a thunder-storm, because he cursed so much. The lightning might strike him, they thought.

When starting to make a drive in the O X Breaks, the boss would caution us not to talk until the first bunch of wild cattle were started. After that, it did not make any difference about talking. Nobody had a chance to talk if he kept up with the drive. He might let out some Texas yells, however. Often the first cattle we saw would be two or three year old outlaw steers. We would sometimes hear their horns crack as they dashed out of the thick cedar brush; they would hit their long, keen horns together, and their heavy, tough hoofs would rattle as they tore off on the rocky hill. I have seen these wild cattle, a few times, walking uneasily around in a bunch of cedars on a high pinnacle far ahead, watching the horsemen approach, but nearly all of them would either break out of a thicket ahead or be running at full speed when first seen.

My first hard race on this work, which ended in a blank for me, came one morning while making a drive on the river. Some of the men had crossed over to the other side to keep the cattle from crossing until the drive could be thrown together, two or three miles up the river, where there was a little open flat right against the bank. Ward Dwight and I were riding in some thick cedar brush close to the river bank, when we heard some heavy animal trotting through the water, which was shallow there.

"That's one of the boys coming across to this side," said Ward, throwing away his cigarette. Then suddenly a big red steer, about five years old, branded on the side, broke out of the cedars so close to me that I could have thrown my hat on his back. Giving that shrill, whistling snort of the wild cattle, he made a frantic leap and lit out across an open flat, running right up the river. Being next to him, I got the first throw, after we had run him at least half a mile. He was a race horse. Being a green roper, I threw too soon, and my loop fell short, striking across his back.

Ward was right at my side, with his loop ready, spinning in the air. He made a perfect throw, but the steer was leaving the ground in a powerful leap when the loop fell right in front of his head. Having both forefeet doubled up as he left the ground, he went through the loop too far, and it pulled up on his hind feet. When the dust cleared away enough for me to see around, Ward's horse was sitting back on his haunches, bracing himself against the rope with every ounce of strength that was in him, and the steer was down in a ditch about ten feet deep and fifteen feet wide. This was the fastest steer except one that I ever saw in that country.

The fastest steer I ever saw passed me on the drive one morning, two or three days later, in these same breaks. He was pure white, about eight or ten years old, and he did not look like he had a scratch on him. He got my horse's wind in the first run and passed out of sight like a ghost. Of course this steer could have been caught in an open country, but that country was so rough and broken that it was hard to get to one after he got a start.

When we tried to get the steer out of the ditch, we found the bushes so thick along the banks that it was hard to get another rope on his head, but the drive came up behind us with some gentle cattle, and Tom Swearingen finally dropped his loop down on the steer's head. They let him get out of the ditch and turned him loose with the herd.

While this was going on, a big, dark red steer, much larger than the one we had, came up over the river bank at a swift trot and loped right by us on the other side of the ditch. As soon as this steer came into sight, Ward got another man to take his rope that was on the ox we had in the ditch and, begging me for my rope, set out in pursuit of the flying outlaw. He was an old steer branded O X on the right shoulder and on the right hip. Another man named George Thompson beat Ward to it. George was riding a powerful blue-grey Figure 9 horse. He got across the ditch first and made one of the finest runs I ever saw, going right up the side of the hill in plain sight. He was close to the old steer swinging a wild loop as they went over the top, and the boys said he caught the big fellow and tied him down before they got up there. The red outlaw steer with white, shining horns that flashed in the sunlight, and the big blue-grey horse, running wildly across the hill, the one for his freedom and the other to play the game as he knew it, made one of the sights that can never be forgotten.

Having gotten the first steer out of the ditch and into the herd, which was brought up and held around him till he got quiet, we drove the cattle up on the hill where the other steer lay with his feet hobbled and his head tied to a cedar bush with George's catch-rope. In catching these wild ones, a man always threw one as quick as possible, then, leaving the horse to hold him, ran to the steer lying broadside on the ground, reached over his back, slipped the loop in the hobble rope over his bottom forefoot, stepped quickly behind him, raised both hind feet a few inches off the ground, slipped the hobble rope under them, gave a gentle shove with the knee, pressing against the brute's hind-quarters, pulling strongly on the hobble rope at the same time, and with a few wraps tied all three legs together. If the animal does not struggle while this is going on, the hind feet will slip forward and the forefoot will slip back from the pull on the hobble rope, and the three legs will lie crossed at the ankles. This is the ticklish part of the job with a big steer—big enough and mad enough to kill you and your horse both—lying there trying to get his breath back so that he can get up and do the job. If the puncher is fast, a few wraps around the crossed ankles and a couple of half-hitches drawn tight with all the muscle at his command, and the job is done. If the man is a little slow, then that is another story.

Anyway, George got down and untied his rope from the cedar bush, fastened that end back on his saddle horn, put the reins back over his horse's head, and backed him off to the end of his rope, where the blue-grey stood with his forefeet braced against the line. Then George dismounted and went back to hold the steer down while another man untied the feet and slipped his rope on both hind feet. Getting back to his horse, this man held the big ox, while George, persuading his horse to slacken the rope, got it off the steer's head and looped it over both forefeet. Now, with rope tight, he ran to his horse. The two men had the steer thus stretched out when some gentle cattle were driven up. Now they eased up on the two ropes, slipped them off their saddle horns and rode off. Jumping up, the big steer kicked both ropes off. Seeing nothing but cattle around, he snorted a few times to blow the dust out of his nose, and savagely hooked some of the young steers that came close to see what he was mad about. Finally, he stalked sullenly off with the rest of the herd.

After dinner that day, Tom Lewis, a man named Estes and I went to help Tom get a cow he had tied down near the wagon that morning. Estes was riding a young horse, and when he walked up to the cow and put the rope on her head, she struggled so hard to get loose, that she scared the young horse. Taking a run on the rope, he snapped it in two at the saddlehorn and went back to camp at full speed. This left me to lead the cow back to the herd tied to the saddlehorn. I was riding a fat little bay horse called Sam, and me and Sam kept out of the way while that cow burnt the breeze, going back to the herd.

Chapter X

Tearing Out of the Cedars

AFTER THE OUTFIT had worked south to the open country north of Paducah, it swung around to the west. We had moved the herd across the south fork of Pease River one morning and camped in a little valley on the north side. The boss put three of us on day herd after dinner. They were making two round-ups a day. Not being able to get many cattle together in that rough country, they would make a drive each morning, cut the cattle wanted, and throw them in the day herd, then make another drive in the afternoon.

There were wild plums on the river. While I was gathering some—and they were fine to eat—the other two men, George Thompson and a man from the Pitchforks, began having trouble with a wild dry cow wearing the Matador brand on her hip. Getting on my horse at once, I rode back to the herd to help hold the cattle. As they were giving no trouble, I rode around to the side of the herd where the cow was providing the entertainment. I got there just in time to see George spread his loop over her horns as she dashed off across the flat. She fell and jumped up again like a rubber ball, and George circled and brought her back full speed, and when she got close to the herd, the Pitchfork man dashed out on his beautiful brown horse and picked up both her hind feet on the run, but when his horse hit the end of the rope, the front cinch broke with a loud snap, the rope came off the saddle horn in some way, the man caught a hard fall, and George was left holding the cow. The big brown horse went pitching and bawling down through the plum thickets towards the river. The saddle had two girts on it, and the flank girt was still fastened tight around his stomach.

George Thompson yelled, "Rope him, kid." It is some job to rope a running, pitching. crazed horse with the saddle turned under his belly I was riding a little black horse called Jumbo, a powerful little brute, but right-handed in spite of anything; that is, he would always run up on the left side of the animal you were after. Finally, at the fourth throw, the loop went right around the runaway horse's neck. He was still pitching and kicking at the saddle when he hit the end of the rope. The back end of my saddle commenced to heave and buck. It was not cinched up tight, but little black Jumbo dug his toes in the sand and finally stopped the big horse long enough to get his breath.

Russ Gregory, who had just come off the drive, saw that my saddle was nearly pulled off over Jumbo's head and yelled, "Turn your horse the other way when he runs on the rope." Sure enough, the brown horse made another lunge on the rope, but now my horse had his back turned to him, and it jerked my saddle back in place on his back. Russ got down and, choking the horse's wind off, walked up to him and unbuckled the flank rig and took off what was left of the saddle. It was kicked and torn all to pieces, except the rigging and the tree. The stirrups and fenders were gone, and the blankets and bridle were gone.

I felt mightily ashamed of this stunt. The Pitchfork man was pretty sore at me for letting the horse tear up his saddle. I should not have tried to rope him; I should have run up and grabbed him by the bridle reins, but, being a green hand, I tried to do what they told me. The man himself was more to blame than any of us, for, as George Thompson told him, "If your rope had been tied hard and fast to your saddle horn, it would have jerked the saddle clear off the horse, and nothing more could have happened."

I never did know how George got the rope off his cow. I guess he dropped it over her hips and threw her to the ground so hard she laid there till he took it off himself.

The outfit worked in between the north and south forks of the river for eight or ten days. This was a mean country to get a wagon through and we would leave it at the same camp for a day or two sometimes, working several miles up and down the river and holding the roundup on any little open flat that was handy. We would make the cut there, bringing it back to the herd. When the grass got short around camp, the wagon would be moved to another water-hole. Drinking the river water was out of the question.

One hot afternoon after we had gone all day without food or drink and were slowly driving a little bunch of cattle to camp, there was lots of talk about the hardships of cowboy life, the blankety-blank dryness of that part of the state, and the general worthless condition of a cow range where there was nothing but salt water in the river and the water in gyp holes in the creeks was so strong it would eat holes in a cast-iron wash pot. Still nearly three miles from the wagon and water, a large young man suddenly dashed off to the mouth of a canyon near at hand, swearing savagely that water he must have. About half a mile further on, two more punchers rode quietly off and disappeared in search of the same thing. Any one of us would have given a dollar for a cool drink of water, but the rest managed to tough it out till we got to the wagon. The three quitters came in later. It always seemed to me that men who did not use tobacco could do without water longer than those who used it, but that might have been my imagination.

After we crossed the herd to the north side of South Pease River, the outfit commenced to hobble a few of the wildest big steers at night. We were working right on their range now, and often some of those we had caught would sneak up to the edge of the herd at night to see what the chance was to make a break for liberty. The men were putting a few big ones in the herd each day, and for a night or two after being "snared" the worst ones were hobbled or sidelined with a piece of new hobble rope.

One evening I saw Jim Thompson and two more men hobble two old steers in the herd after sundown. It would be hard for anybody of the present day to realize how large and strong these old steers grew up in the breaks of those salt water rivers. Jim was a Matador peeler, and he was lucky in two ways. He caught both those tough oxen, one at a time, and the last one when it was nearly dark, and did not get hurt. But Jim had a dandy Matador horse and was a top hand anywhere himself. As Ward Dwight said that night, "What difference does it make if they do jerk your horse down? There is plenty more horses."

Ward and myself stood first guard on this trip and he and "Tinker" Williams and Jim Thompson hobbled these old outlaws while I rode around the herd to keep the cattle together. They did not run these wild cattle any more than was necessary, but the instructions from the boss were to hold them in the herd if possible until the outfit got to the railroad, where they would be loaded on the cars and shipped to the packers at Chicago.

Jim Thompson rode in the herd first, while the other two men watched on the outside with their ropes down, so they could catch them if they broke out without letting them get away very far. As luck turned that way, Jim caught the first steer in the herd, and letting him gradually pull the powerful Matador horse, by the weight of his giant body on the end of a thirty-five-foot, 7/16 inch hard-twisted sea-grass rope, with the other end tied to his saddle horn, Jim soon eased him out to the edge of the herd, where Ward picked up both his hind feet. I could plainly see the dark forms of the riders and hear the creak of saddle leather as the grim old fighter made his last furious struggle and sank to the ground stretched out with two good horses holding him down. He was the larger of the two steers, and Tinker soon had a brand new piece of hobble rope tied from one front foot to one hind foot, short enough that he could walk but could not run.

They let him up, and Ward went in the herd, but the other steer saw him coming and ran out by Jim Thompson, who caught him around both horns as he dashes by. Tinker caught him by a hind foot while I helped Ward hobble him around both forefeet. It being then about dark, the other boys turned him loose, while I loped back around the cattle to see that none were straying off. Ward soon joined me on the night guard and the other boys went back to camp.

These two steers were both branded O X on the right shoulder and O X on the right hip. It was called the Double O X brand. Ward told me the company had quit using this brand about ten years before; they were now branding the single O X on the right side, using the old mark, an under-bit in each ear. This would make all of these Double O X steers ten years old or older, and there were lots of them still in those breaks.

The outfit had tried putting a winter camp in the breaks, with men and grain-fed horses to catch the big ones, after they got thin in the winter, but they could not be handled at all without a good-sized bunch of gentle cattle to go along with them, and no fence had been built that would hold them. They might stay in the pasture a day or so, but they would jump any kind of fence at night and travel back to their old haunts in the rough canyons on the river.

Contrary to many magazine articles and fiction stories, these steers were not the thin-chested, slab-sided, knock-kneed scalawags so often pictured as the old-fashioned Texas cattle. They had long, keen horns all right; that part of the popular idea is true;

but these cattle were fine upstanding brutes, mostly red, red-and-white spotted, and roans in color, showing their descent from the big red bulls that had been turned loose in the river breaks years before. Some of these bulls had died; others had grown up and gone wild. It was a case of the survival of the fittest, the process of selection being aided to some extent by man. The cowboys often let a big, fine bull calf escape the knife because "he was a fighting fool and could take care of himself."

Many of the stock raisers of that day wanted cattle "that could whip a loafer wolf," and there were lots of big steers and bulls running loose in those old rough canyons that could do the job and then some. The outfit did not hobble many of these steers, only about ten or fifteen, on this work, because it took up lots of time to hobble them at night and then turn them loose the next morning; it was killing work on the horses, interfered with us getting an early start on the drive, and, after all, did not do much good. After we thought they were located and quit putting the hobbles on them, we could see their tall forms even at night in the herd, and if a guard was not close, when one walked to the edge, there was a rattle of hoofs and usually a vain chase on a pitch dark night. Although it is possible to see cattle grazing off from the herd on a star-lit night for a short distance, one cannot see clean around a herd of two thousand cattle at night unless the moon is shining. The outfit generally worked a range until they gathered about that number, taking the shipping stuff to the railroad, or taking them all to the shipping point and shipping what was desired; then the others would be taken back to the home range, the calves branded, and turned loose.

There was no pistol practice while the outfit was at work. It was my privilege to work under three good bosses that summer, with three different wagons, and there was only one gun play started. It would have been lots of trouble to carry a pistol, belt and cartridges, buckled on the waist all the time, and do the work that these men had to do. Mr. Arnett, Sherman Swearingen, Tom Benson or any of the boys would have laughed at me if I had told them to get their pistols and shoot in front of a stampeded herd at night. Shooting would only scare the cattle worse, if possible. If five or six men on good horses will run to the lead as soon as the cattle start running and stay there in front a while, the cattle will soon get over their fright, and will slow up enough to be turned or milled around, until they forget what it was that scared them.

Chapter XI

Roping Old Ball and Twine

FOR THREE OR FOUR DAYS after the trouble we had on day herd down on the South Fork, my spirits were at a low ebb, on account of the awful bust I made in trying to rope the horse that got loose with the saddle, and because the other men could beat me roping so bad. With this outfit were eight or ten older men who were dandy good cowmen, like Mr. Brazile, and good workers who never tried to rope the wild stock, although they would go in a herd sometimes and rope calves when the outfit was branding, or they would catch a calf once in a while for meat. Eight or ten younger men were experts at roping the wild steers. I wanted to be a roper, but it looked like I would never learn to rope well enough to catch one of the wild bunch, or even get a chance to catch one. These men hardly ever missed. If one of them ever saw a wild steer quit the drive and make a dash to get away, he would catch him the first throw, unless, as sometimes happened, the steer outran his horse or the horse fell down with him.

It was the custom for the ropers not to crowd each other, and they always gave the first man after the steer a chance to make his throw. Lots of times there would not be but one man after him, though sometimes two or three would see him get away. Always one would go to help if he saw a man leave the drive after a big fellow, as everybody knew that was dangerous work.

Sherman Swearingen, having the wagon boss job for the first time, was anxious to make good on this trip, and he got us up early and worked hard all the time. One morning we left camp on the river to make a drive five or six miles north and then circle back towards the river, where the wagon was camped in a valley. The sun was barely up as we rode out of the canyon into some little cedar-covered ridges and hills covered in places with loose lime rock and gravel. Hardly had the men in front reached the top of the first ridge, when there was a loud noise, such as heavy animals make when running over loose rock. Then a bunch of wild cattle broke out of a cedar thicket ahead of us and dashed madly away. There were three big steers and seven or eight cows, calves and yearlings in this bunch, and we could plainly hear the old steers' horns crack as they almost knocked each other over in their haste to jump out of the thicket and be gone.

Two or three of the men took after them, and they soon headed the cows and yearlings, turning them back into some more cattle. These hills were full of cattle that had watered at the river the day before and were now grazing on the good mesquite grass that grew in the lime rock country. Finding plenty to do here, I helped on the drive for quite a while, and we had taken the cattle back into the broken hills near the head of the canyons running out from the river, when we came up on a little rise and saw ahead of us two men on top of the ridge, about fifty yards off, with a steer tied down on his side in the brush. I was up close to the point of the drive on that side and rode up to them. It was Tom Swearingen and George Thompson, and they had the daddy of all the big steers in captivity.

Riding up to him, I gazed in astonishment at the huge brute. He was red-and-white spotted in color, pale red alternating with pure white. He was branded a long irregular stripe commencing on his neck on the left side, running down across the left shoulder, with a big B A T on his left side. They called it the Lightning Bat brand, and he must have been the first steer calf that ever wore it. This steer must have been at least fourteen years old, and his huge body and long gleaming horns, as he lay there on the ground, made a startling picture. George and Tom had him tied by the horns with a doubled lariat rope to a strong cedar bush, and they had one of his hind feet tied hard and fast to his hind leg above the hock on the other side. I was so amazed at the size of the huge brute, I did not ask which one of them had caught him, but their horses both looked like they had been in a race before they got to him. The boys said he was one of the three big steers we jumped first that morning.

Taking the cattle on, we drove them a few miles further along the ridge, until we met the boss and some more men, who had been making a circle to the north of us, bringing in more cattle. They had a good sized bunch, among them six or seven big "oxen" they had managed to circle and throw into the drive without roping them. As it was about noon, time to get back to the roundup ground, the boss told us to point the drive back by the steer that had been tied down that morning and that they could untie him and take him along with the herd.

We were driving them along quietly enough, when I saw Ward Dwight, who was riding right behind me, leave the herd on a little dun O X horse at full speed. He was dragging an extra big loop. Looking ahead on a little hill, I saw the big Lightning Bat outlaw just getting up. Not knowing he was so close, I had not seen him until Ward started. Another man on the other side of the cattle was going after him too. Before they got to him, the wild ox broke the hobble rope that was on his hind feet, and when he got up, he broke the double lariat rope that anchored his head, dodged in between the two cowboys and dashed off down the hill. However, Ward was soon riding at reckless speed close to his side. When he roped him, the old rebel jerked the little dun horse off the ground. Being a full blood cow horse, however, he lit on his feet, with all four feet set to hold. The big steer whirled around and almost lost his footing as the next man caught him by the hind feet. They stretched him out. We had brought the herd pretty close to where the men were working with the old steer, when I heard a vicious snort behind me, and turning in the saddle, saw a wild-looking red-roan steer, branded what they called the Ball and Twine, a round ball high up on his hip with a long crooked line running from the ball down his hind leg.

He was walking nervously towards the edge of the herd, shaking his head and looking straight at the men who had the spotted steer roped, not more than thirty or forty steps from where he stood. Seeing that he was getting restless, I and another man next to him took our ropes off saddle horns and, popping them aganist our boots, rode up towards him, thinking to "shoo" him back into the cattle. Raising his head proudly, old Ball and Twine looked squarely at first one of us and then the other. He never backed a step. Then suddenly, with a snort of anger, he lowered his head and dashed between us, scattering men and lime rock as he went. As they all do when they get a chance, he made for a canyon near. Loping off into it, we found a wide ditch in the bottom, much too wide for a horse to jump and too steep to cross right there, but the red-roan steer leaped it in a single bound, and head up, trotted lightly away, up the far side of the canyon.

There were three men followed this steer, and when he jumped the ditch in the bottom of the canyon, they all lit out up the ditch, to find a place to cross. While standing there on my horse, I happened to look down the canyon and saw a good place to cross about twenty yards below me. Thinking that here might be my chance to do something, I rode down, crossed the ditch, and was soon on top of the side of the canyon. Red Jim, one of my best young horses, was under me that day, and we had not been in a hard race either; so I knew he was fit and fine. Looking both ways, I could not see the steer, but I could see two men coming from up the ridge riding like madmen.

I knew they could not pass Red Jim with the start he had, and, touching him with the steel, I loped out on the ridge, where I could see little spurts of dust fly up over the low cedars going down towards the river.

Certain that this was the big steer, I gave the horse his willing head, and Red Jim fairly flew down that divide. Much to my surprise, when I came up in sight of the steer, a cowboy named Estes was right behind him. He was swinging his rope. My heart sank at the chance I had lost, but I did not slacken speed as Estes might need me to help get him down. My horse was running at full speed on a loose rein. Getting nearer, coming over a little rise, I could see that the other man's horse was spent, that he had just made a throw and had not been close enough to catch.

This gave me a throw, and, running with smooth and even stride, my horse put me right up by the side of that flying ox. He looked much taller and bigger than my horse, but when I caught him around the head, he plunged forward to his knees, jerking my horse a considerable distance forward. This gave the big steer a lot of slack in the rope to play with, and he reared up on his hind legs and dashed off towards the edge of the canyon. I had two girts on my saddle, both of them drawn tight, and when the next jerk came, my horse set his feet firmly as he hit the ground. Old Ball and Twine came to his knees the second time, and as he rose up again, Estes rode up and roped the steer around the horns to keep him from fighting, and we tied him up between two cedar trees so he could not run on either rope. The other two men had got there by this time, and they turned out to be George Thompson and "Tinker" Williams, two of the best ropers with the outfit. Estes told them he was not there when I caught the steer.

They looked at old Ball and Twine, as he threw

his powerful body against the two ropes that held him prisoner, and then they looked at me and my horse, but I think Red Jim took most of the credit in their eyes. He was a fine-looking dark bay, and carried himself proud, as I rode him slowly around to quiet him down. He was a smooth-running, speedy horse, and would go up on either side of a brute, was easy reined, and never stumbled or fell down on any kind of ground.

As the herd was still out of sight, we rode back up the ridge and met them, and when we got back in sight of the big roan steer, he was right where we had left him tied up between the two cedars. Estes and George Thompson rode ahead with me to get him ready to turn loose in the herd. We untied the ropes from the cedars, one at a time, putting my rope back on my saddle horn so I could hold the steer while Estes untied his rope from the cedar and tied it back on his saddle horn. We played the outlaw steer out on an open place, where George roped him by both hind feet. As the cattle came slowly up, some of the gentle ones walked all around us. As George gave me the word, we both slipped our ropes off the saddle horn at the same time, dropping them on the ground, and rode quietly out of the herd. When the big steer jumped up, we were gone. Kicking the loose ropes off his feet, he walked sullenly off through the herd. As the cattle moved away, we picked up our ropes, and old Ball and Twine moved off up in the lead. He did not leave the drive any more.

Chapter XII

With the 9 Wagon

∿∿

MR. BRAZILE AND I worked with the O X wagon until they got back to Childress, where we cut out our cattle and took them back to the camp at Brazile's place. The last glimpse I had of the O X men, they were driving a bunch of the big steers with some gentle cattle into the shipping pens at Childress. I could see two or three of the old rebels lying tied down outside the pens on their broad side, and two or three more were doing their best to outrun a bunch of cowboys and get back to Pease River. All the wild steers were shipped regardless of brands, as they all had owners who were anxious to get rid of them. The money they brought was sent to the different men who claimed the brands.

When we got back to Mr. Brazile's place, I found that the owner of the brand I represented had made a contract to sell all he could deliver by a certain time to two cowmen living at Childress, Givens and Lane, as I recall their names. They should have made some money, as cattle were awful cheap at that time. In a day or two Ward Dwight came by from the O X outfit on his way to the Figure 9 wagon, at work near Quanah. I was sent along with him to gather as many of our cattle as possible, to put in on the contract the owner had made with the men at Childress. We found Will Lanier and Tom Davidson already with the 9 outfit. The camp was only four miles south of Quanah.

While at this first camp, the only approach to "gun play" I saw all summer came off. There was with this outfit a stray man, called Buckhead Billy, because he worked for a man who used the Buckhead brand, a crude likeness of a buck's head, burnt on the side of the cow. Tom Benson, the boss, was in town, and some of the boys, amongst them Buckhead Billy and Tom Davidson, had been to Quanah. As there were no cattle to look after that night, things became rather boisterous. There was a lot of drinking, card playing, swearing and cutting up generally all over camp. Just before supper, while the sun was yet about an hour high, Buckhead, who was about my age but very strong and bull-necked, got into a "wrestling match" with Tom Davidson, the Figure 8 man. They both felt "funny," and grabbing each other, laughing and talking, they clinched. Round and around they went, upsetting beds and falling over saddles. They were both strong as bulls, and finally they both got mad, the bad whiskey in them doing its worst. Finally, Tom spun Billy around off his feet, and threw him flat on his back right in the middle of the camp.

Furious at this public defeat, Buckhead Billy leaped to his feet and, swearing destruction, death and damnation against his opponent, ran to his bed, which was lying unrolled nearby, jerked a .38 caliber Smith and Wesson revolver from it, broke it open, and commenced to throw some cartridges into the cylinder. Just as he started to snap it back and get up, I saw Tom's face grow dark and hard. Taking a couple of quick steps, he leaned over the boy and wrenched the sixshooter out of his hand, at the same time pushing Billy back into his bed with no gentle hand. Tom stepped back, picked up the sixshooter, threw all the cartridges out of the cylinder, and flung the revolver as far as he could after them. Taking a stand over the bed, he proceeded to tell Buckhead a lot of things that I could not understand, but managed to make out that he wanted Billy to crawl in that bed and stay there until time to round up the horses the next morning.

Nobody saw Buckhead any more that night, and it was generally thought he did what Tom told him to. Of course Billy could have crawled out of his bunk that night, hunted up his gun and killed Tom Davidson, but he was not a mean boy, and when the bad whiskey died in him, I am sure he did not want to kill anybody and saw that he was wrong. Buckhead Billy was brave beyond any doubt, for he would get on the worst horse they could lead out, without the flicker of an eye lash.

During the work, Jim Williams found one of his saddle horses that had been gone for over a year with a bunch of wild mares on the range. We got these mares in the remuda, and Jim roped his horse, led him out, and telling us all that here was a real pitching horse, one that would throw any man in the outfit. He asked Billy to ride him. The boy never hesitated a minute, but said, "Wait till I turn my horse loose." He was on horseback at the time. Jim's horse was a beautiful brown, fat and clean-legged and as supple as a panther. Billy rode with two girts, and when they eared the horse to put the saddle on, the boy stepped in his tree without untracking him. Then he leaned over the saddle horn and struck both of his thumbs in the horse's neck just in front of the shoulders. This made the ride start quick, and the brown horse went higher off the ground at every jump, for four or five jumps, and then settled down to some of the fanciest pitching that any pony could do. Billy came back grinning when the show was over, and Jim told him to keep that horse and ride him for a few days.

Buckhead Billy was, next to Marion McGinty, one of the best bronc riders in that country. He could ride without holding or "grabbing leather," or he could lean over on one side, holding the saddle horn in one hand, and spur any ordinary horse from his shoulder to his flank, with the other foot out of the stirrup, as long as he wanted to pitch.

To get back to camp, after the excitement over the wrestling match had died down, we had supper. Having some desire to go to town that night, I got to talking to a couple of men with the wagon who wanted to go, and they gave me such a glowing description of the night life in Quanah that I decided to go with them. They said they knew a place where the music and dancing was not to be equalled in any town on the Denver Railroad. After their descriptions of the beauty and accomplishments of some of the fairer sex they were acquainted with at this place had worked my spirits up to a high pitch, we all three decided not to lose any time going. My two companions cautioned me that it would not be necessary to call each other by our real names, but we could use the brands of the cattle we represented on the range as a title when addressing each other and talking to the guests. Also this would be convenient in case the affair got in the papers. We did not know each other's names; so no one's reputation would be injured and there would be no notoriety, unless there was a funeral. One of my friends was a small sawed-off puncher, with only one eye; he was nearly as small and runty as myself, and called himself "Four Spot" because he was working the Four Spot brand. The other was a veteran cowhand, a fine singer, also a mighty poker player; he was an R 2 man, and there was nothing to do but call him R 2 for the night. As for me, as the R 2 man said, nobody knew my name anyway, as every one called me The Kid. Getting these matters settled, we were soon at town, where, after a bath, shave, and purchase of a new necktie, we got on our horses and were soon at a little dance hall near the edge of town.

Anyone over twenty-one years old, except the habitual drunkards, could buy all the whiskey he wanted. The saloon men usually would not sell them more than a quart. We did not buy any whiskey, as we did not go down there to get drunk and disorderly. I did not have a Colts 45, myself, and if either of my friends had a six-shooter, he did not display it. After going inside and blinking our eyes to get used to the light, I was taken around by my friends and introduced to the ladies.

There were two girls that my companions assured me were full-blood Indians. They were the musicians at the dance, and both of them could sing and play on the banjo and also dance very well. They were good-looking girls, the older about eighteen, and the younger about fifteen, years old. We all danced and sang several vocal selections in which the R 2 man played a prominent part. After dancing until a late hour, I got one of the little Indian maids to pin a large yellow chrysanthemum on my coat, while the other two cowboys were getting a similar decoration. Then we reluctantly took our leave.

The next morning after leaving camp, Tommy Davidson discovered the yellow chrysanthemum, which I had entirely forgotten, still pinned on my coat. Bawling like bulls, coughing and uttering terrific bovine snorts, he and five or six more of the younger men dashed their horses up around me, and, spurring furiously on all sides, tried to snatch the flower from my coat. Whirling almost from under me, my frightened horse tried to break through the circle of bawling cowboys. Knowing that it was just horse-play and that they wanted to have some fun, I dashed about, trying to out-dodge them. Finally, after a lot of running, spurring and frantic dashes, they hemmed me up and Tommy unpinned the flower from my coat while running at full speed. Proudly then, he pinned the big yellow chrysanthemum, on his own coat, and rode along, looking down at his shadow on the ground. Mirrors were scarce and hard to get to, and if we wanted to see if our appearance was correct, we usually looked down at our shadow on the ground as we rode along. All the boys joked me about the little Indian girl for a day or two, but I did not mind it. A puncher has to get used to lots of jokes.

We commenced work as soon as the wagon got to

the river and worked on south to, and all around the town of Crowell. It was just a small place with a livery stable, a couple of stores and post office. A kind of milk-weed with a broad leaf growing on one straight stalk, having a cluster of white flowers, when it bloomed, right at the top, grew on the flat country. It was from eighteen inches to three feet above the ground, in scattering bunches, sometimes two or three plants close together. Sometimes ten or more plants could be seen far away on the prairie. When looked at far off through the shimmering heat waves of a broiling summer sun, they were easily mistaken for a solitary coyote, a couple of motionless antelope, or even a bunch of these animals, especially if there was a mirage near them at the time. This weed gave out a thick sticky liquid-like glue. When a leaf was broken off at the stem, this milky glue would run out and drip slowly to the ground. This substance bothered our horses a good deal. They would get it on their muzzles while grazing at night, and wherever this liquid touched them on the face or nose, it formed a blister, the flesh becoming very tender and the hair coming off.

After all the strays were cut out of the roundup each morning, the herd would be grazed till after dinner. Then that evening we would help the Figure 9 men brand their calves. In this way all the 9 cattle that were gathered in each day's roundup had their calves branded and were turned loose, as they were right on their home range. Nothing was held in the day herd except the stray men's cattle and the dry stuff that the outfit intended to sell that year.

On a drive near Crowell, Will Lanier roped an old salty brown cow, with a big set of horns, as she ran off from the roundup. Another man rode up to catch her and help get her back in the herd, but Will, who was riding a powerful, heavy-bodied, red-roan horse, branded Z on the left shoulder, shouted to him, "Don't rope her, I've got her." About that time the old cow made a dash between them, running two lengths of the rope, and when she hit the end of it, the girt broke like a shoe string. Will always rode with one girt. As the saddle was jerked from his horse's back, Will fell to the ground. Another man standing near with his rope down made a quick throw and caught the old cow before she got away with Will's saddle, which had the twine tied hard and fast to the horn.

Another day while we were penning a bunch of cattle at the 9 pens, south of Crowell, a wild two-year old heifer ran off. Buckhead Billy, who was already in the pens helping build a fire, borrowed a horse from Tom Lewis, the R 2 man, that was standing tied to the fence. This was an old sorrel cutting horse. He carried a double-rigged saddle with saddle pockets, which some punchers still kept on their saddles. There was a dirt tank right at the pens, small mesquite bushes growing all around it. The wild heifer beat Billy to the tank. Running around it, he was crowding the horse to get close enough to rope her, when she dashed into the water to cross. Buckhead was spurring to the limit when the old sorrel, who perhaps decided there was no way to please this man, downed his head, bugged out his eyes, and went into the tank right behind the heifer, pitching and bawling like a wild bronc, scattering water, and popping the saddle pockets so loud the whole outfit stopped to watch. He could not loosen Billy in the saddle, but he scared the heifer so bad she ran into the pen with the other cattle.

Having gathered quite a lot of stray cattle by this time that belonged to us four men, Will Lanier, Tom Davidson, Ward Dwight and myself, we decided to cut them out. There were about 250 head, a pretty good haul for two weeks' work. Tom Davidson and I drove them to Brazile's place.

Chapter XIII

Broncs and Broomtails

〜〜〜〜〜〜〜〜〜〜〜〜〜〜〜〜〜〜〜〜〜〜〜〜〜〜〜〜〜〜〜〜〜〜

AFTER COMING IN with these cattle, I stayed around camp for a couple of weeks, helping Mr. Brazile get our cattle shaped up for delivery to the Childress buyers. It seemed odd to me to stay around a house after having been out with the chuck wagon so long. One day word came that Will Lanier had got sick and left his horses and bed with the 9 wagon. I returned to that outfit to take his place.

Ward Dwight, Tinker Williams, Buckhead Billy and several Figure 9 punchers I knew were still on the work. Among new men was a lad called the Wild Dutchman. He was a black-haired, black-browed, fat, heavy-set kid, with more skill with the lariat than I have ever seen in any other boy of his years. Ward told me there had not been a big steer caught on the drive in over a week. He said, "There ain't no more big steers left this far down on the river. There ain't nothing down here to rope but calves and these damn broncs that Buckhead and Dutch are breaking. They are getting our gentle horses all skinned up, dragging the broncs out of the remuda on horseback, because they are so wild they have to catch some of them on a horse to keep them from running off with the rope."

What worried me was that mount of fat horses Will Lanier had left for me to ride. He was a fine rider, and I knew that most of his horses had been thumbed in the neck, on both sides, every time they started to pitch with him. As I looked them over, the boys told me that he rode the worst one in his mount off when he started home. They were all fresh; some of them had not been ridden on that work, and they were all fat as mud. I had never ridden a bad horse in my life, but two or three of the boys said they would help me if anything happened. After riding all but three successfully, I tackled a big dark bay horse, branded a half circle over the 65 on his left hip. This horse would really go high and pitch hard. While Shug Reynolds rode up by my side to grab him in case he went to pitching too hard, Jim Stout eared him down till I got on him. The big horse snorted, gave one high leap over against Shug's horse and trotted off. Shug said he sure was scared for me when old "Ida," as they called him, made that first jump.

The safest way to ride a young horse is to give him a good hard ride the first time you get on him, and when I got in off the drive that morning with Ida, he had quieted down a whole lot. When his turn came the next time and he saw that I did not "goose" him in the neck with my thumbs or spur him in the shoulder, he got gentle right away and never did pitch after that.

There was a little cream colored dun pony in my mount with a white mane and tail and yellow eyes, branded V A N on the left hip. He was rather a harmless looking horse, but the men said this was the worst vinegaroon in my mount. He had thrown Joe Todd, a noted rider, and if he could not throw his rider, he would rare up and fall back on him. Knowing that I had just ridden what they called a bad horse and got away with it, I decided the boys were joking. When I roped the dun out of the remuda, he led as gentle as a dog. As the girts were tightened he merely flinched. This should have made me suspicious, but as he let me saddle him by myself I took the catch rope off, tied it on the saddle and stepped into the saddle without untracking him. Then with a squeal, Dunny jumped straight up into the air as high as he could go, tying some kind of a knot in his back as he hit the ceiling. The second jump sent my hat spinning to the ground. The third jump found my right hand still holding the bridle reins and also securely fastened in the hair of his mane, while my left hand was down on the point of his left shoulder. By main strength and awkwardness I pushed myself back into the saddle, got hold of the horn with my right hand, and with the bridle reins in my left I rode that chunk of blasting powder until the squeals finally died out and he quit pitching. This horse got his head down all right, but I had the horn, which made us about even.

Having learned to cuss a little by this time, I rode up to the men who were standing around and said, "I want to see some of you blankety-blank peelers who yelled so loud for me to hang 'em in him ride this horse, right now, and spur him. I've got money that says you can't do it." No one took me up. I was sore across the stomach for a couple of days. I liked the big bay Ida horse fine. He was a smooth, easy-riding horse and had lots of sense. The C 5 sorrel, which did not pitch, was always crazy. Somebody must have beat him up pretty bad when he was broke. The little dun horse had a peculiar kind of a stiff trot that was very disagreeable to ride. Although none of the horses gave me any more trouble beyond the necessity of watching them and holding their heads up for the first fifty yards of a cool morning, it was a daily relief to me to get in off that work without any broken bones.

Along in August it began to rain again, mostly at night. The outfit had worked south to the Big and Little Wichitas. There was lots of water in the little creeks, and the cook generally camped the wagon close to a little water hole of fresh rain water. One night he camped by a hole about forty feet long and about eight feet wide. It was customary on dark cloudy nights for the cook to leave the lantern burning, hung on the back end of the wagon, so that the men coming in from guard could see to find camp. This trip Jim Stout, the stuttering man, and I stood guard together, and that night we staked our horses on curly mesquite grass the other side of this little pool.

Some time in the night, everybody was called to go to the herd, on account of a big rain that was coming. It did not rain so much, but the lightning was bad, with lots of electricity in the air. There would come a blinding flash, and the soft blue white-looking balls of fire would dance on the horse's ears. A little shivering flame would play along the backs of the cattle, jumping from one to another. It would disappear and burst the next instant, into little balls of fire on the tips of their horns. The cattle drifted a good deal, and it took about two hours to hold them until the storm passed over and get them back near the wagon again. Then all hands except the regular guard went back to the wagon.

Jim Stout and I had a hard time finding the camp, but after riding in circles for quite a while, we spied the glimmering lantern. Riding up, we staked our horses, and stumbled through the darkness towards camp. Jim was ahead of me just a step or two, and, dazed by the lantern's shining in his eyes, walked off into the pool of water. Although I was nearly walking in my sleep right behind him, the loud splash and the fierce stuttering oaths that boiled up from the pool warned me to stop. Fully awake, I ran around the other side of the pool and, reaching down my hand as a dark figure waded to the bank, I helped Jim pull himself out, while he filled the night air with a fresh burst of hip-hop profanity.

Buckhead Billy while running his horse at full speed in front of some of the drifting cattle that night crashed into a barbed wire fence. The noise he made when he hit the fence turned the cattle and started them to milling around, but his horse was so cut up that he bled to death before daylight. Billy was thrown clear of the wire and was unhurt.

A few days later while we were making a drive, Ward Dwight and I saw a band of "broomtails" coming out of Pease River bottoms. The 9 outfit had lots of these stockhorses in two different brands, the L 7 and the Teaspoon. The last was a crude device to represent a recumbent teaspoon, burnt on the left shoulder. The horses were not real mustangs, but mustangs could not have been any wilder. As the sun was just coming up, we watched the broomtails race across the prairie, and Ward said to me, "A sorrel pony in that bunch looks like the horse you lost while we were working down here last spring."

"Yes," I returned, "and if he has two white hind feet, it is my horse." I galloped out on the prairie to get a good look at them. They scattered and broke into a run, and my bald-faced sorrel horse, with two white hind legs, came into plain view.

Determined to "find out where he went," I took after them. Knowing that running wild horses is entirely different from running cattle, I let my horse, an old sorrel we called T I D, from the brand on his hip, take his time. He was the kind that never quits, and I knew he could run them down some time that day. There were eight or ten head in this bunch, most of them dry mares, and a big black horse that looked like a stallion. My horse was the only sorrel among them. Old T I D was fresh and wise. He knew what he had to do, and kept up a steady gait about half a mile behind them.

After the second mile, they slacked up, and I gave old T I D the spur to see how much speed they had. We got pretty close to them but they had lots of speed. They ran through a bunch of ten or twelve antelopes grazing on the prairie, scared off a big buck from the main bunch, and he was still jumping around stiff-legged and looking silly, as goats will look, when I passed him. Seeing that I did not have near enough speed to head the wild horses yet, I kept in behind them at a long easy lope for a good while. They were

Sketches

by

Carl P. Benedict

Pet Hawk
drawn at Midland, 1912

Blue Dog, favorite horse
drawn about 1898

Prairie Dogs and Owl, Midland County, 1912

HALFBREED BUFFALO COW

One morning in the spring of 1895, TX cowboys making a roundup on the Pecos River brought in an old TX cow followed by a little heifer calf that was evidently out of a buffalo bull. They branded the calf TX(T on the left side and X on the left hip) and turned it loose to grow. While she was still a heifer, R. D. Benson, owner of the TX Ranch, sold her to the Cowdens and she was taken to the TA Ranch, owned by Cowden and Waddell, twenty miles south of Midland.

At the time I first saw the cow, in 1908, when she was thirteen years old, she was still on this TA range, though it had changed hands. She had raised only three calves, one of which had died, but her three-year-old steer and two-year-old bull were alive and thrifty. She stood about eighteen inches above other grown cattle and thus loomed up plain clear across any herd at any time. She was never still, but would walk restlessly around among the cattle in a herd, watching cowboys cutting out the cattle. If one got close to her, she would trot over to the other side. She weighed about 1300 pounds, but was as smooth and graceful in her movements as a deer. No fence could hold her. When she grew tired of a certain pasture, she would jump the fence and leave for a while, but would always come back to the old TA range. She was finally shipped with her increase, the steer and bull, to the Fort Worth market.

I saw her many times and made a sketch of her in 1908. In 1923 I made from the sketch the painting here reproduced.

heading towards two little twin hills, or pinnacles, sitting out on the prairie. I made up my mind that if they ran close enough to these pinnacles, I would try to point them between the two, hoping the rocky ground there would slow them up while I would try to beat them around one of the peaks, and turn them back towards the wagon, now far to the east across a level prairie.

Sure enough, they ran between the two peaks, the old black leading the way. Throwing the reins down loosely in my hand, I leaned over and gave old T I D the steel. He ran around the south peak on the level ground, and we were looking at them when they came out from between the two pinnacles on the west side. The big horse gave a loud snort, and whirling around the south side of the hill they were off like the wind to the east. The old sorrel, still game as a buffalo, struck a long lope, and we set out to run them back to the wagon.

My horse was still breathing easy, and running at half speed with a slack rein, I knew he had the "change" for this bunch, though they could have still outrun me if they had been crowded. They were much easier to keep up with going back than they were on the first run, and when we got in sight of the wagon, the wrang had the horses spread out grazing all over the flat north of camp. The wild bunch ran straight for the saddle horses, but the wrang, who was in camp when they came in, jumped on his horse and did his best to keep them away, as he did not see me coming in behind them. Riding far out to one side, galloping first one way and then another to attract his attention, and waving my hat frantically, I at last got his attention. Then he let them come into the saddle horses.

The men were working the roundup about a mile from the wagon, and the wrang and I watched the horses until they got through and came to camp to eat dinner. When the horses were rounded up for the catching of fresh mounts, the big black proved to be not a stallion, as I thought, but a six or seven year old L 7 stag that had never been broken. He had been running loose on the range all his life. Crowded up in the remuda, Buckhead Billy and another man called "the wild Dutchman" roped him around the neck, on horseback. He fought like a panther when they dragged him out on the flat, and when he choked down, they hobbled him with a brand new piece of hobblerope doubled and twisted good around the forefeet, and staked him with a stake rope to a bush. I caught my little sorrel. His name was Shiloh, and he was branded 7 DL on the left hip. I rode him that afternoon. He was as gentle as a dog, and I was glad to get him back in my mount. After the men had all caught fresh horses, they cut the wild mares out of the bunch, and ran them off.

The boss, Tom Benson, told me he was awful glad to get the black L 7 stag, as they wanted to break him. He gave him to Buckhead to ride. He already had a mount of wild sugar-eyed broncs he was breaking. But he never rode the big black, for they broke his neck the next morning when they roped him to take the hobbles off.

Chapter XIV

Comrades

〰〰〰〰〰〰〰〰〰〰〰〰〰〰〰〰〰〰〰〰〰〰〰〰〰〰〰〰〰〰〰〰〰〰〰〰

A FEW DAYS AFTER I recovered the sorrel 7 DL pony, Ward Dwight and I cut our cattle out of the day herd and set out for Brazile's place. We got to a deserted pen, about half way, close to sundown, and had the worst time two men ever had trying to pen those cattle. There was nothing but a little cedar rail pen, big enough to hold maybe three hundred head. It was built on an open place, and had one short wing running out from the gate about thirty steps. This wing allowed the cattle to circle clear around the corral. We had about two hundred head, with five or six old wild cows and some two-year-old steers among them. We could run them up close together, and by riding hard we could drive them right up to the gate. One of the wild cows would always be in the lead; then, looking in the gate, she would give a loud sniff and tear out, taking most of the cattle with her. When this happened, and it happened six or seven times, one of us would have to stay and hold the cattle that did not run off, while the other brought back the ones that got away. Ward and I took it time about, bringing them back.

By dark we had most of them in the pen. Then a bob-tailed two-year-old steer stuck the stub of his tail straight up in the air and darted off, taking about twenty head with him. Yelling to Ward to watch the gate, I took down my rope and whipped that steer around the corral twice. I was riding the little sorrel Shiloh pony, the fastest in my mount, and when the bob-tailed steer dropped his stub of a tail and broke away through the mesquites, it did not take us long to catch him. Ward said that when he rode up, I was standing on the ground, trying to beat that bob-tail steer to death with my rope. He said he sure thought I was killed when he came to hunt me, as there were some awful holes around that pen, and it was getting too dark to see. Ward had shut the gate, nearly all the cattle being in the pen. Turning bob-tail loose, we drove him to the other cattle that had run off and put them all in a little horse trap, or pasture, near the house.

The cattle woke up several times that night, walking about the corral and hooking each other with their long horns. We made our bed down close to the corral gate, after staking the two night horses and hobbling the rest and eating a little snack. The cattle would have had to run over us to get out the gate. The morning star came up on time, and it did not take us long to broil some bacon and boil coffee in an old tin can, to down with cold biscuits.

I rode the big bay Ida horse that morning. Ward offered to bet me a dollar that I could not spur him and get away with it, but we did not make the bet. He flinched and snorted a little when the saddle was eased up on his back, but I held him carefully while girting the saddle on good, patted him on the neck and led him off a few steps to open the gate so the cattle could come out. By the time they were all out of the pen and I had shut the gate, my horse had the kink out of his back and trotted off like an old cow-horse. No one ever called me a bronc rider. There are lots of things one can do, if he wants to, that will keep a horse from pitching. Like many of his kind, Ida was all right after you trotted him off fifty or sixty yards in the morning, but if he was dashed off suddenly, as quick as the rider mounted, he would "call" for his man, every time.

Soon after we left camp that morning, we got up in the cedar brake country, and the five or six old cows kept giving trouble for a couple of hours. They were not so wild as they were just mean and contrary. They always walked up in the lead, and when they reached a brushy place, they would slip into the cedars, and one of us would have to lope up to the front and turn them back. Sometimes one of us would ride in front for half a mile, holding them back. When we dropped back to the rear to help drive the rest of the cattle, we had to keep a sharp eye to the front. However, the farther cattle are driven, the better they behave. Our old cows were behaving well when we reached Brazile's that evening. Will Lanier had got well, and he came over and helped us shape up my employer's cattle for delivery to the Childress buyers. We got together about 700 head of stock besides the calves, delivered them at $10 around for the cows, calves not counted, $11 per head for two-year-old steers. The bob-tailed steer had stayed in the bunch and he was behaving himself when I saw him walk past the bosses counting the cattle out on horseback.

Soon after this, we got word that the 8 wagon was coming up through Crowell and Mr. Arnett was going to work through the Witherspoon range and gather the rest of the 8 cattle and get all that Tom Davidson and the rest of us had gathered that summer. Getting everything ready, Will Lanier and I again set out, with two mounts of horses and a bed roll. A remnant of cattle in our brands were still to be picked up. I knew this would be the last work of the year, as it was nearly October now and they did not work late in the fall in that part of the country.

We found the 8 wagon near Crowell, and all the boys that had been with them in the spring were still along. Cap Weatherly and his brother Harry, Mc-Ginty, Mr. Arnett, Cal Lowry, the cook, and the rest of us all had a big time telling jokes. Ward Dwight had come down to work with us through the river range, and he told the boys all about the trouble I had with the bob-tailed steer. I had grown to be very fond of these men. In the spring I had started out such a "tenderfoot" that I did not know how to tie up my bed roll; now I felt that I was making a pretty good hand. I knew that any of the men would have killed a good horse to help me in case of trouble. We worked for a couple of weeks through the flat country, and were just going up into the hills, when the blow fell that put an end to my good times. We had just made the "Copper Mine" roundup, so called because something called an old "mine" was near the roundup ground.

I was coming in from the herd with some of the other men to change horses, when Mr. Brazile's nephew, Tobe Brazile, rode out from the wagon and told me that his uncle had bought the remnant of cattle we were gathering and that my employer had sent word for me to come in and bring my horses to Mr. Brazile's place. Knowing that this was the last of those happy days, it was with a heavy heart that I caught a fresh horse and walked up to eat my last meal with the chuck wagon. I could not talk much and when the time came to say good bye, it was hard for me to look like a wild, bad cowpuncher.

Ward Dwight was the last man I spoke to. He shook hands when I told him good bye, we looked at each other, and I turned around and rode off feeling that all the joy had gone out of my life. As Ward had helped me cut my horses and drive them away from the remuda, it took but a few minutes for me to put them in a steady trot.

When I got about a half mile from the wagon, I turned once and looked for a long minute at the men working with the herd on the open prairie, at the wagon with the cook going around washing the dishes, and at the wrang taking his horses out to find the best spots of grass to graze them on. That night I rode into Mr. Brazile's place and the next morning started back to the "lower country," as they called the settlements.

For a long time I did not see any of the boys that worked up there. Some of them I have never seen. I have never been back to that country, and do not want to go back, because it would be painful to me to see the open prairies where we used to throw the roundups together, now cut up into farms, and to hear farmers' cow-bells jingling in the Pease River breaks where once we chased the big, free steers.

Chapter XV

Cutting Horses, Range Bull Fights, Lobos

vvvvvvvvvvvvvvvvvvvvvvvvvvvvvvvvvvvvvvvvvvvv

OLD HUB

OLD HUB, of the Figure 8's, was the best-known and the best cutting horse that worked in the herds over the big range country his outfit was a part of. A fine looking dark bay, branded HUB connected on the left shoulder and the Lazy 8 on both hips, he was about 15 hands high, very heavy muscled, with short-coupled, powerful body, clean legs and fetlocks, with feet well shaped and small for so large a horse.

Contrary to an old belief that top cutting horses were all Spanish or drawn from the native mustang breed, Old Hub was a blooded horse. What line of breeding he had I do not know, but not far behind him must have been some noted mare or stallion of the saddle horse or Thorobred strain, from back in the blue-grass country. No one ever saw a horse or stallion of the work-stock breeds in that country. Horsemen all wanted horses to ride, and when a man rode up to the wagon with a mount of horses from any of the big ranches, like the Pitchforks, Mill-Irons, Matadors, 8's or the S M S, it was a pleasure to look at his mount of picked horses. The cowhands were given the best. The misfits, the auger-eyed outlaws, and horses that had no cow sense were sold or shipped east for work stock.

There was no better horse in any man's mount than Old Hub, then in his prime of life, about ten years old. He had been with the 8 wagon as long as Mr. Arnett, and he had been Mr. Arnett's favorite cutting horse for several years. As Bud Arnett had been wagon boss for a long time, he handled lots of herds and cut cattle daily all the time. Old Hub got lots of practice, and, trained by a master hand, he became almost human in his ways. I used to sit on my horse, watch them work in the roundup, and wonder if it would ever be my luck to ride a horse like that.

Bud Arnett could cut wild yearlings out of the herd as long as they came, without a bobble. Old Hub would take them to the edge of the roundup and dart them out to the cut before they could bat their eyes. He could take a young dry cow, the hardest of all brutes to cut when they get cranky. Hub would step carefully around through the cattle, so as not to disturb the roundup, until he coaxed her to the edge, and then, with lightning speed, he would play with his forefeet, dashing them at her, first on one side and then the other. If she whirled back, he would be between her and the herd. If she ran, he would keep just the right distance behind her, for he had so much speed that no brute could outrun him, and with his eyes watching her every second, he would turn as the cow turned, stop as she dodged, and jump sideways to turn her back towards the cut. Finally, when she gave up and started to go, Old Hub, with flashing eyes and waving foretop, would "walk on her heels" until one of the men working between the cut and the herd would come to put the brute in the cut.

Turning slowly, he would fox trot back into the herd, and bring out a nervous young cow, with her first calf, as patient and calm as if he were jogging back to the wagon for dinner. Watching carefully, he would keep the mother cow pointed to the edge of the herd, gently stepping behind the little calf occasion-ally so it would see its mother and go forward. When they got to the edge of the roundup, he would gently scare the calf up to the cow, and when she turned to leave, he would drive it behind until it followed the mother off.

In short, this fine horse was known and admired by every puncher who worked with the 8 wagon in his time. He had made and kept his reputation by hard work on every dusty roundup ground in the gyp water country from the Double Mountain River on the south to Pease River on the north. It was gener-ally known that Old Hub had never let a brute get back in the herd within the memory of man.

In August, 1898, four years after my trip to the range country, the second annual Cowboys Reunion was held at Haskell, Texas, still a cow town on the eastern side of the caprock on the plains. This was the second year that contests had been held by the cowmen for the benefit and amusement of the ranch boys, themselves, and their families. Anyone could enter by payment of the small entrance fee, and there were no "professionals," only regular ranch hands. The first cowboys reunion known in that section had been held at Seymour, Texas, the previous year.

At the Haskell reunion, Mage Smith brought in a herd of 1000 head of range cattle from one of his pastures near town. A choice lot of bad pitching horses was gathered up from different ranches, and a bunch of big outlaw steers was brought down from the Salt Fork River to give all the ropers a chance to show their skill. I will not attempt to describe all the roping and riding contests. Commercial riders and ropers have made them familiar from New York to San Francisco, although there were stunts pulled at that reunion unknown in the arenas of today.

The cutting contest, as my memory clings to it after so many years, was an extraordinary offering for the entertainment of a crowd. I can see as if it were yesterday the cowboys bringing in that 1000 head of cattle and rounding them up in front of the grandstand, about nine o'clock in the morning. Ten horses and riders had entered in this contest. Mr. Arnett had consented to let the Figure 8 boys bring Old Hub and enter him in the cutting contest. They, like the other big outfits, brought their own chuck wagon, grub, beds, and remuda. It was no trouble to bring old Hub along. He was now about fourteen years old, and when I saw him once more and looked at his proud carriage, the noble and beautiful head, and the heavy muscles moving under his velvet coat, it was not hard for me to decide which horse would be the winner.

The other horses, all but two or three, drew places before Old Hub. Each rider with his horse was to cut 100 head—so many dry cows, so many steer yearlings, and so many cows and calves. This variety would test the skill of each horse in cutting the different classes of cattle. There are many horses that can cut single cattle much better than they can cut cows and calves and vice-versa, but it was considered that the champion should do the best in all classes, with any extra flourishes he could throw in for the judges to pass on. Every horse in this contest was a chosen favorite out of the top cutting horses from the ranch that entered him. Nobody was allowed to make more than one entry. They were all splendid horses, picked for their cow sense, speed and powerful, smooth action on the roundup ground.

As I recall, "Boley" Brown, on a fine sorrel horse from the 24 Ranch of Scoggins and Brown, near Clairemont, Kent County, Texas, took second prize, and "Cefe" Cummings of Haskell took third on a five-year-old brown horse. Another man pulled his bridle off and cut a few cows. When Sam Graves, one of the Figure 8 peelers, who was the lucky man picked by Mr. Arnett to ride his old favorite, went into the herd on Old Hub, there was many a cheer from the boys of his home range.

Stately and proud, the veteran commenced working out his cut. As if working under ordinary conditions on the roundup grounds of the lonesome range, he never paid any attention to anything but his work and though the cattle acted nervous and frightened by the huge crowd of people gathered around, it made no difference to Old Hub. As is usually done on the range, his rider cut ten or twelve cows and calves first, as they will stay in the cut better when it is started than dry stuff that is wild and fat.

Having got his number of cows and calves out with care and faultless "cow work," Sam commenced

*Sam Graves and Old Hub, Cutting Horse,
at Cowboy Reunion, Haskell, Texas, 1898*

bringing out the dry cows, Old Hub working them to the edge of the herd with perfect strategy and graceful action. Sam wound up with the wild steer yearlings. It was a joy to see this fine cutting horse work them on slowly to the edge, and then show his wonderful speed and matchless headwork as they tried futilely to outdodge him and then to outrun him to get back in the herd. After he had cut the allotted number, without a single error that the most critical spectator could see to object to, a roar of applause swept the grandstand. Next, as each entrant was allowed to do if he could, Sam Graves pulled his bridle off, rode back into the herd, and cut ten more dry cows. As Old Hub, without a bridle, brought them out without a single error, the crowd went wild.

Riding quietly away, Sam Graves joined the rest of us men who had taken part in this contest, and waited until the other contestants had completed the exhibition. These horses were all good cow horses. After they finished, all were called up near the judges' stand. Then Old Hub got a fine blue silk ribbon tied on the headstall of his bridle and was declared the Champion of the Cutting Horse Contest. When Sam Graves rode him slowly back by the grandstand with the blue ribbon fluttering in the breeze, many a wild cowboy yell rent the air for the gallant horse and his rider.

It might be worthy of note that Jim McGinty, a thirteen-year-old boy, drew a horse in the pitching horse contest that had killed a man and rode him successfully. In another event, Matt Walker roped one big spotted steer from the Salt Fork, on the "Jim

Bailey" horse (a beautiful big dappled grey) and tied the steer while the horse pitched clear around him with the rope tied hard and fast to the saddle horn and Jim Bailey ran out of the grandstand on foot, yelling, "Tie him, Matt! Tie him! The horse is all right!"

THE STORM

To have the opportunity to watch Nature and the animals, wild or tame, that have to live in the great outdoors and battle with the many different perils that come to them in such a life has always pleased me much more than to watch the works of man. The noise of a large city, the clash and rattle of tin against tin, the grinding of steel, the screeching auto horns, the stench of burnt lube, and the reeking smell of gasoline have no pleasant effect on one who has spent years in the open.

Although some of the modern youth, sons and daughters of the great millionaires of today, might say they would not give one week of their life in the bright lights of a great city, riding around on the soft, luxurious cushions of a powerful car, frequenting the gay night clubs and palatial mansions of the rich, for a century of life such as mine, yet to me there is pleasure in just the memory of the soft, deep-toned lowing of a distant herd of cattle. There is no discord in Nature's artillery, when the black clouds of a Texas storm come piling up over one's head, amid a stillness and darkness that seem as if a mighty spirit were riding aloft and directing the fury of the elements.

I remember the pale glare of the lightning, followed by terrific crashes of thunder, as one bolt after another fills the pitch blackness of the night with liquid fire, then the first gust of wind that drives some cool drops of rain into my face as a welcome relief, while the cattle drift off the bed ground and riders gallop visible in the vivid and constant lightning flashes, loping along by the sides and in front of the herd to keep the cattle together. A rain storm at night always made me think of the power of God over the world, in the good old days when many people believed in heaven and hell and in a reward for the just in paradise.

The Loafer Wolf

Much has been written about the vocal powers of our friend of the prairies, the coyote. But for the true wilderness music, music that will reach deep into the human system and make a man sleeping on the ground in a lonesome camp, with or without company, raise his head and listen, there is no sound like the full, deep-toned howl of an old male lobo, or "loafer wolf." They used to walk out on the cedar-clad hills at night, in the red breaks of the Salt Fork, along the Wichitas and up the canyons on Pease River and raise their blood-stirring cries.

They are not so generous with their music as the coyote. It used to be they would rarely howl more than once or twice in a night, generally about 9 or 10 o'clock, after good people had gone to bed. But what they lacked in quantity, was fully made up in quality, for when the lobo raises that wild, deep, blood-curdling call of his in the dark, all the coyotes barking within three miles of the spot stop suddenly, and bark no more until their dreaded kinsman makes his night's meal and goes back to his lair.

Despite the power of the lobo's wild and lone-world howl and of the mighty bellowing of the old range bulls, the purest and sweetest music I have ever heard is that coming from the regular beat of a running horse's feet on firm ground.

Bull Fight at Roundup

If one desires to watch an exhibition of sheer brute strength, coupled with the Nth degree of fury and blazing courage, let him go with me back to a summer day on herd with the 8 wagon, and watch a combat between two of the big range bulls, as they lived their life in the year 1894.

Slowly, as they recognize the strange voice of a new bull in the herd, three or four of the big wrinkle-necked red bulls that have been in the day herd for a couple of weeks begin to circle around through the cattle, stopping often to paw up the dirt, throwing it up on their backs, meanwhile giving tongue to their savage and deep-chested bellow.

All the while, the new-comer, thrown into the herd that morning with a "cut" from the morning's drive, stands his ground. Turning slowly around, always keeping his head to the foe, he shows the most dangerous front of them all. A little smaller than some of the bulls, he is solid red of a yellowish cast on the body, running to dark blood red on the neck, head and lower parts of the hoofs on all four legs. Built with round, heavy muscles that stand out in folds all over the brute, his heavy spike horns with needle points setting slightly upward from the head, his eyes under shaggy front gleaming with the deadly look of the "killer," this bull promises plenty of fight.

Approaching steadily, the other bulls select, as if by common consent, one of their number to do battle. A huge old bull with scars of former combats on his neck and shoulders stalks forward. Other cattle in the combat zone swiftly slip away.

Turning their heads partly to one side, the two adversaries bow their necks and, stepping lightly sideways, move silently forward as if marking the distance. Suddenly, with furious snorts, each whirls on his hind feet and charges straight for the terrible horns in front of him. The shock and the loud crack as horn meets horn is plainly heard by two cowpunchers sitting on their horses about a hundred yards away. At the moment of impact the two huge bodies are in the air. The shock stops them both momentarily, but the superior weight of the old bull bears his opponent backwards fifteen or twenty feet.

Seeing how his mighty foe can outdo him by main strength, the spike-horned fighter keeps his horns pressed with every ounce of his weight against the foe, head still against head. Then, as quick as a flash of lightning, he leaps to one side, charges with deadly skill, and gores the veteran behind one ear with such power that he almost flings him to the ground. With a savage roar, the big bull whirls with lightning speed and catches the young bull under the neck with both

horns, throwing him clear of the ground and back-
ward.

Nothing daunted, the spike-horned bull lights on
his feet and without a moment's pause charges savagely back. Again it is bull head against bull head.
The fierce crack of their horns shatters the silence of
the quiet summer afternoon. The big bull can throw
the young one back at every charge, but he can not
catch him before he whirls back, head on, to the
battle.

Finally, making a furious lunge and feint at the old
bull's head, the young bull leaps to one side, catching
the brave old fighter behind one ear. Savagely, he
bends the old one's neck to one side. Suddenly
changing his stroke, he drives those deadly horns
under the big bull's brisket, throws him fairly broadside to the ground, cutting skin and flesh to the bone.

Near exhaustion, the killer bull rocks on his feet
for a moment to get his breath. The old warrior,
sensing the chance for escape, slips from under those
spike horns and runs for his life, the victor following,
slashing at his flank. He is seeking to disembowel
him, but the stroke falls short. The deadly horns cut
the empty air. Out of breath, the savage brute stops
and reels drunkenly on his feet as breath comes in
gasps from his mighty lungs. Gazing with red and
blood-shot eyes towards his other foes, he grimly
starts back to the herd. His assaults have been so
powerful, so skilful and deadly that no other bull
comes forward. He is acknowledged victor even
though he has not killed.

There is no end to the memories that flood me when I get to going back to the free range over which I rode so free with other free young men so long ago. Often there comes to me the hot scent of the cedar brakes, the boys tearing out of them on sweat-lathered horses behind the stretched-out wild cattle. As I rest in my chair, I can close my eyes and see the look of eager delight that used to come over Ward Dwight's dark face when a big snuffy steer left the drive. He could build a loop in behind one of those outlaws quicker than any other human being I ever saw. No man ever loved the game better than he loved it, and few were as good at it. No movies could handle those big steers the way we handled them. If they tried, the stars would all have the seats of their pants hooked out. Was there ever any other kind of work so filled with the eagerness of high-hearted sport and with such good comradeship?